Praise for

# REDESIGNING CAPEX STRATEGY

"Must-have book for those who need to redesign capital allocation and capex strategies."

**—GUSTAVO WERNECK,** President & CEO, Gerdau

"Having implemented the 'Weissenrieder' process in a material and successful way, I was very pleased to see Fredrik and Daniel publishing an easy-to-understand book to be passed down through our organization. It will forever change how you and your team think about capital management!"

**—HOWARD COKER,** President & CEO, Sonoco

"Fredrik and Daniel have developed an approach to assessing and prioritizing long-term capex strategies capable of having a meaningfully positive financial impact for decades to come. We have actively deployed their approach to capex allocation and have executed investments that are creating real competitive advantage."

**—STEPHEN SCHERGER,** EVP & CFO, Graphic Packaging International

"Why not to challenge our capex allocation processes? Are we really exploring important points with a long-term view? This book brings a new approach to the capex. We at Klabin were well pleased with the results after two projects with Fredrik and Daniel, both with involvement of our team, data mining, generating ideas and options, having thrilling discussions on scenarios and opportunities, and generating great results!"

**—FRANCISCO RAZZOLINI,** Executive Director & CTO, Klabin

"This book, and the related practical work process, provide the critical missing link between capital expenditure planning and corporate strategy."

**—ALEXANDER TOELDTE,** Chairman of the Board, Clearwater Paper

"The simplicity in the methodology has helped us to focus on company cash flow and long term strategy. We have a much better understanding of the relationship between investments and long-term shareholder value. The book is as the methodology—easy to read and easy to understand!"

**—HENRIK SJÖLUND,** President & CEO, Holmen

# REDESIGNING CAPEX STRATEGY

# REDESIGNING CAPEX STRATEGY

## A Groundbreaking Systems Approach to Sustainably Maximize Company Cash Flow

### FREDRIK WEISSENRIEDER
### DANIEL LINDÉN

Mc
Graw
Hill

New York  Chicago  San Francisco  Athens  London  Madrid
Mexico City  Milan  New Delhi  Singapore  Sydney  Toronto

1  2  3  4  5  6  7  8  9    LCR    27  26  25  24  23  22

ISBN       978-1-264-28529-7
MHID       1-264-28529-9

e-ISBN    978-1-264-28530-3
e-MHID    1-264-28530-2

This publication is designed to provide accurate and authoritative information in regard to the subject matter covered. It is sold with the understanding that neither the author nor the publisher is engaged in rendering legal, accounting, securities trading, or other professional services. If legal advice or other expert assistance is required, the services of a competent professional person should be sought.
—*From a Declaration of Principles Jointly Adopted by a Committee of the American Bar Association and a Committee of Publishers and Associations*

**Library of Congress Cataloging-in-Publication Data**

Names: Weissenrieder, Fredrik, author. | Lindén, Daniel, author.
Title: Redesigning capex strategy : a groundbreaking system approach to sustainably maximize company cash flow / Fredrik Weissenrieder & Daniel Lindén.
Description: New York : McGraw Hill Education, [2022] | Includes bibliographical references and index.
Identifiers: LCCN 2022011942 (print) | LCCN 2022011943 (ebook) | ISBN 9781264285297 (hardback) | ISBN 9781264285303 (ebook)
Subjects: LCSH: Cash management. | Business enterprises—Finance.
Classification: LCC HG4028.C45 W45 2022 (print) | LCC HG4028.C45 (ebook) | DDC 658.15/244—dc23/eng/20220311
LC record available at https://lccn.loc.gov/2022011942
LC ebook record available at https://lccn.loc.gov/2022011943

# CONTENTS

Foreword   vii

## PART I

## Today's Flawed Approach to Capex

1   DELTAS VERSUS DOLLARS   3

2   FROM ISOLATED PROJECTS TO INTEGRATED SYSTEMS   29

3   A ~~GOING~~ *GROWING* CONCERN   57

4   CAPEX NEEDS VERSUS CAPITAL ALLOCATION OPPORTUNITIES   69

## PART II

## The Wiser Way to Capex

5   THE STARTING BLOCK   93

6   CREATING A CAPEX STRATEGY MODEL   115

7   THE BASE ALTERNATIVE: STRATEGIC ASSET MAPPING   131

8   THE BASE ALTERNATIVE: CASH FLOWS   141

9   STRATEGIC BUILDING BLOCKS   153

10   STRATEGIC ALTERNATIVES   163

11 **SENSITIVITIES AND LIMITATIONS**                 177

12 **EXECUTION**                                      185

---
PART III

# Capex as an Economic Catalyst

13 **SUSTAINABLE DESTRUCTION**                        197

Afterword                                           209

Acknowledgments                                     215

Index                                               217

# FOREWORD

I'm antibusiness books. Most of them, anyway.

When Domtar Corporation was a public company and part of the Fortune 500, as the CEO I would have maybe 50 books like *Redesigning CapEx Strategy* land on my desk a year. Most of them you dump. With one or two of them, you think, *Oh, I'll read this*, and you never do. I may have opened one in five years.

Business books have the bad habit of taking the particular and turning it into something so general that it doesn't have any implications for the rest of us. I would see the word "revolutionary" on some of these book covers where the content just recycled some of the same ideas or methodologies from elsewhere. The books tended to oversell themselves.

This book, however, undersells itself.

It's easy to miss the revolutionary aspect of Fredrik and Daniel's methodology, but it is nothing short of radical. This book is about more than "redesigning capex." It's about transforming the way you look at capital allocation and seeing that you're completely wrong. It's about realizing that capex strategy is the enterprise's strategy. The way corporations and capital-intensive industries deploy capex right now is nothing short of a train wreck. Outside of Weissenrieder's clients, no one looks at their asset base as a collective network. They see their assets as stand-alone performers and the same thing with their capex opportunities. They have no specific strategy for the role each asset plays in the grand scheme of things. Because they have no strategy, they have no idea how to invest in their network for the long term to generate more cash for the business, asset by asset.

Capex thinking is driven by the concept of returns. If the internal rate of return (IRR) on capex X is twice as good as capex Y, you'll choose capex X. If that's the way you see the world, you'll overinvest in bad assets and underinvest in the best. You'll spend a lot of money through the years, and then be surprised when, in the end, you're generating no cash and eventually go bust. The worst assets show the best paybacks. Your strong assets will show lower returns because they're already strong performers. Your perspective will be to invest money in your worst assets, and this will go on until eventually, through neglect, your best assets will lose cash flow and start performing poorly, too.

It's a question of throwing good money after bad.

Fredrik and Daniel have developed a methodology and the tools to enable you to see the whole range of potential strategies and cash flow outcomes for hundreds of scenarios across a multi-asset base. It's extraordinary and nothing short of dropping a bomb in the world of capital allocation. This is not about incremental improvement. It's a radical transformation of how you allocate capital.

I was Weissenrieder & Co.'s first customer when Fredrik formed the capex strategy consultancy. At that time, I oversaw the Swedish company SCA's packaging operations in the United Kingdom. We worked together again after I became the head of its European packaging division with 10 mills and 70 plants. Because of their credibility in the pulp and paper industry, I should not have been surprised when I moved to Domtar to become its CEO and found Fredrik already there, timeless taste in fashion and all. I, of course, continued our relationship.

Over the past 20 years, this is the type of faith I've developed in Weissenrieder & Co.: I keep the capex strategy they developed for Domtar in my top desk drawer. Whenever I have an important decision to make, I take it out and ask myself whether the decision is aligned with our long-term strategy.

The one time we ignored their advice, with one particular mill, we have hemorrhaged money because of it. We've been trying to backtrack on our ill-fated decision ever since. I daresay we would have saved a hundred million dollars on just this mill. We learned our lesson.

That gets to the point, really. The kind of clarity Weissenrieder provides is extraordinary. Before going through the process, everyone has their own opinion on the company's plan for allocating capex. Even if you think everyone's bought in, if the 15 people in the room were being honest, each one of them has a "Yes, but—" mentality. Sometimes people passively disagree with the overall plan. After Weissenrieder's process, you're left with no choice—you have to face reality that mill X might not have a future, even if mill Y has a bright one. Everyone's talked about it and has their opinion, but afterward there's no question.

This book shines a light on a sordid little secret that, actually, a lot of capital allocation is based on emotion. It's not fact-based. There are capex analyses, but those are seen as just a tool, if you will, as part of the decision-making process. With a capex strategy that accounts for each individual asset's role as part of the asset network, there is no question as to the best path forward. It's as plain as day. *Redesigning CapEx Strategy* doesn't just redesign your capex strategy. In the process, you redesign your entire company's future.

It's difficult to grasp how powerful this clarity is, from the board all the way to the mill floor. The mill manager understands not just their own role but the role of the mill in the company. Most would say their role is to keep the place alive and running, regardless of ownership or the network in which their mill operates. With this level of clarity, they see how their mill plays a much larger part inside the greater company. Whereas before they might say, "I need $100 million every year, but they only give me $10 million," they're now aligned with the overall strategy. I've seen companies spend tens of millions on outside consultants and not achieve this degree of clarity.

There's also clarity about the role the company itself plays in the big picture. I chair the advisory board for the Stern Center for Sustainable Business at New York University, whose motto is "A Better World Through Better Business." I am proud that Domtar's capex strategy has led to substantial gains in creating a more sustainable supply chain, that our company has become an active leader in being the solution to the problem—not a passive contributor. The more sustainable our business is, both environmentally and financially, the more sustainable we enable our customers to be.

Domtar's motto is "Making Life Better, Every Day." I feel that is precisely what these consultants' process has done for us. As I've followed Weissenrieder's work from afar over the past 20 years, I've seen the same thing in multiple companies and even other industries. The profound change at all levels is truly remarkable.

I have the greatest admiration for what Fredrik and Daniel are doing. I believe their book is going to be a godsend to other CEOs and all of those who work with the capex process, from the shareholders to the greater stakeholders.

**John Williams**
CEO, Domtar Corporation

# PART I

# Today's Flawed Approach to Capex

# DELTAS VERSUS DOLLARS

When the leaderships of industrial companies put together their capital expenditure (capex) budgets, they may have capex projects with an average discounted payback period of three to four years. If undiscounted, perhaps six months sooner. This is an impressive return, far beyond their investors' expectations. If a capex project's expected life is 15 years, investors are OK (presumably) with a discounted payback in year 15. By leadership's estimates, however, the investors can expect a payback in just three or four years.

Over several years, this type of performance provides the investors with an enviable total shareholder return (TSR), much greater than that of a general stock market index. Such a high TSR signals that the company's leadership knows how to sustainably allocate its capital optimally, make money from those decisions, reinvest its cash flow well, and provide dividend growth that comes from earning cash more quickly. Such a company would be the shining star that everyone is talking about.

If we were to graph a curve that represented the sum of this industry darling's capex projects contained in next year's capital budget, it might look something like Figure 1.1.

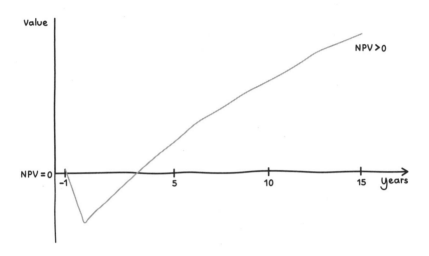

The sum of all the company's capex projects is plotted as an accumulated discounted cash flow curve. While the curve goes downward, cash is going out. Then year one has a positive cash flow and the curve starts its upward journey. After three years, the average capex project has earned back the company's capital investment, including the capital cost. Every year thereafter is putting money back into the company's coffers, either to be distributed as dividends or perhaps to be reinvested in this stellar performer's operations. At these returns, after a decade, a company valued at $10 billion today could become a $1 trillion company.

Of course, in reality, this doesn't happen. Perhaps the company's price estimates were wrong. Freight costs rose more than expected. The timing is off. Projects come in over budget and take longer than originally planned. Let's say that all of this doubled the original payback period, from three years to six.

No matter: a collection of 15-year capex projects that earns back its capital investment in six years to begin generating a positive net present value (NPV) is an impressive accomplishment. This still results in a TSR well above the stock market index and will continue for decades to come. The board of directors will applaud the CEO year in and year out. The CFO will be invited to every conference as the company's peers eagerly await the knowledge of how the company became so successful. The company itself becomes the industry benchmark with its pick of talent.

Regardless of whether it is for companies with 3- or 6-year discounted paybacks—or even 8 or 10—this fantasy doesn't transpire. In fact, such companies often perform well below expectations on the stock market. How can companies continually have capex plans that deliver such results, yet those numbers never result in company performance? Mathematically, how is this possible?

It's not . . . and reality bears this out. Companies that routinely require such short discounted payback periods routinely deliver a disappointing performance on the stock market. These very companies often have a distinct lack of cash flow, distressed financials, an insufficient capital budget to operate the company long term (much less take advantage of growth opportunities), and little-to-no increase in distributed dividends . . . year after year after year. Their TSR, shall we say, leaves something to be desired.

> Sitting in his office, the CEO of an American steel company once told us, "I know all the numbers are right. But after approving our capital expenditure plan for next year, my gut tells me something's wrong. We're missing something somewhere."

The reason these industrial companies experience this paradox is because of the way leadership calculates capex projects' benefits and the way capital budgets are decided. They are disconnected from how the company actually generates cash. At best, there is no correlation between how they measure capex projects' performance and company cash flow; much more likely, there is an *inverse* correlation. Just as Europeans didn't question Ptolemy's theory for around 1,400 years that the Earth sat at the center of the solar system, the professionals steeped in capex processes have never questioned one of its most basic assumptions—that there is a mathematical correlation between what they measure and what they want.

Industrial companies' capital allocations are primarily the result of a number of purely tactical decisions. Capex projects aren't considered in the broader perspective of the development of the total production footprint, customer expectations, the overall marketplace, the company's long-term strategy, and other such crucial facets of a successful business. This is especially troubling considering industrial companies' success rests almost solely on a handful of major capital allocation decisions made over the years. An ineffective (or, in most cases, inexistent) capex strategy leads to exactly the problems we've just described.

With the benefit of hindsight, we can go back and calculate the discounted paybacks from a number of heavy industries' performances. While forward-looking analyses promised perhaps a 3-, 6-, or 10-year payback period, Figure 1.2 shows the historic aggregate performance of those capex projects.

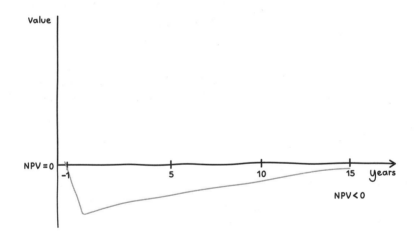

The actual payback?

Precisely never.

This graph isn't theory; its data is a matter of public record.

Spending capital is at the heart of a company . . . and the way it's spent now is like plaque that is slowly building up in your arteries year after year. The company's leaders continue to approve capex projects that continually promise results that are never realized at the company level, in the company's cash flow. This is a disaster financially, economically, socially, and environmentally. A financial disaster for its company, an economic disaster for its country, a social disaster for those whose lives are affected, and an environmental disaster because inefficient methods of production are perpetuated instead of being updated and upgraded.

The majority of drivers believe they are better-than-average drivers. The American Automobile Association (AAA), for example, released a study showing that 8 of 10 men in the United States believe they are above-average drivers. Put another way: 80% of US men believe they're in the top 50%—which would mean 20% of the group makes up the bottom 50%. Obviously, the math there doesn't work out. Likewise, in the majority of companies the leadership believes it is made up of better-than-average managers. Even their companies are special, while the others are not. Obviously, reality doesn't bear this out. Without objective measures, however, there is no evidence to show that the leaders of any particular business are the exception to the rule. Some are better than others, but that doesn't mean they're good.

We've worked with the leading companies in a number of industries across the world. It's been our experience that there are dramatic gains to be made from identifying and capitalizing on the capex opportunities hiding in every production portfolio we've ever seen. The primary difference between the conventional approach to capex (used by 99% of industrial companies today) and ours is focusing on production as a holistic system instead of a series of individual capex analyses. Many people are jaded when it comes to the word "holistic," so let's define exactly what we mean.

Our method is holistic in that it includes the entire company (or group, division, etc.) in one comprehensive capex analysis; a whole capex calculation in one go, if you will. It focuses primarily on sites' and the total system's capital allocation opportunities—not individual capex requests. Because it's based on actual company cash flow, not the change in cash flow, there is a direct and clear connection between the analysis and actual cash.

It's holistic in that it's not "owned" or run by the operations, manufacturing, or strategy people. It is created by a cross-functional team that represents the best resources from sales, marketing, procurement, logistics, manufacturing, engineering, finance, and more. A holistic approach necessitates such involvement because the company's capex strategy touches every aspect of the organization. This team considers asset capabilities, market position, demand, customer preferences, raw material supply, engineering opportunities, and so on.

It's holistic because it's not time constrained. A capital budget, for example, is only valid for a period of time. Usually a year, though multiyear budgets aren't unheard of. Our approach effectively designs the company for the next 10 to 15 years (and sometimes even longer). While the capital budgeting and capital management processes are still necessary, they become secondary to the overarching capex strategy from which all other company decisions derive.

Instead of a reactive approach to capex needs (which is, by and large, how most companies operate), a company should be driven by a proactive, long-term strategy designed to take advantage of the unique opportunities within (and often outside of) an existing portfolio of facilities.

The senior vice president of strategy at one of our largest clients once told us that doing the calculations of our process wasn't rocket science, that anyone with Excel could do it. While we think it's a bit more complicated than that, his next words got to the heart of the matter: "The value you guys brought to our company was in educating us on how to look at capex performance completely different from how anyone in the company had ever looked at it before." Once the leaders embraced this holistic way of evaluating capital allocation decisions, it transformed their company.

All it takes is avoiding the obvious mistakes (well, obvious once equipped with the right lens) and making a few more correct decisions instead. Then, continue to do so for a few years, eventually resulting in superior company cash flows and, for our publicly traded clients, performance superior to that of their peers on the stock market. The positive effect on company accumulated discounted cash flow will be in the range of a 20–100% increase. We know because we've been developing this method since the mid-1990s and can track those clients' performances.

To echo the Foreword: it is nothing short of a radically different way to view capital allocation.

## MORE EFFICIENT CAPITAL ALLOCATION

Capital expenditures make up more than 20%* of the average country's economy. Unfortunately for the world, companies analyze capex projects the same way they have since the 1960s. They've had to; they had no other choice. When corporations began formalizing how they allocated capital between projects, they borrowed cash flow discounting techniques developed for the financial markets. Theoretically it made perfect sense. Applying it to individual project requests was efficient from a data-processing point of view—important in an era where computing was expensive and programming difficult.

At the same time, because companies' profit margins were so high, there wasn't an economic incentive to even consider a better alternative. Besides, what they were doing was working. Because this was the only way to approach capex, business school professors taught generations of corporate executives that this was the one and only way to approach capex.

---

* The term capital expenditures, or capexes, is being used here in the broadest sense, looking at gross fixed capital formation, including business, government, and consumer gross fixed capital formation.

There are two reasons this is unfortunate. Today's technology allows for a more in-depth way to calculate the impact of capital budgeting decisions. Computing power costs less and is more accessible, giving us greater tools to use in calculating capex costs and benefits. For instance, instead of running massive Excel spreadsheets across multiple workbooks like the two of us did years ago, our team now rents computing power from the cloud at a fraction of the cost with exponentially more processing power. Simply put, we can crunch a lot more numbers a lot more quickly. Today's capex analyses don't have to be limited by the computing power available, giving us far more options. We don't have to accept what we've been given, but being taught the established approach to capex blinds people from considering these other options.

The second reason the 1960s approach to capex analysis is unfortunate: it's based on analytic thinking instead of systems thinking, and that is what we'll be talking about in this book. When a capex project is submitted, it's considered in isolation. Typically, the company has metrics each project must meet, such as a maximum payback period or to clear a certain hurdle rate. It comes down to pass/fail criteria for capex projects: If a project meets the minimum requirements, it's put forward to be considered against all the other proposed capex projects. If not, in most cases it's rejected outright. The underlying assumption is that approving only "good" projects results in a better company. However, this often results in an "efficiency paradox." This is when optimizing the parts of a system leads to an overall suboptimal system.

We think of it as the "Moneyball paradigm." In the book *Moneyball: The Art of Winning an Unfair Game,* author Michael Lewis showcases how a Major League Baseball team, the Oakland A's, made history in 2002 by winning 20 games in a row. In the movie by the same name, there's a scene where the owner of the Boston Red Sox tries to recruit Billy Beane, the A's general manager responsible for the historic streak. The Red Sox owner says, "You won the exact same number of games that the Yankees won, but the Yankees spent $1.4 million per win and you paid $260,000."

That is, Beane was five times more efficient with his team's capital allocation decisions than the fabled New York Yankees. Put another way, the Yankees' general manager wasted 80% of his team's capital by sticking with the old tried-and-true method instead of adopting the same approach Beane had.

The Red Sox owner then said, "I mean, anybody who's not tearing their team down right now and rebuilding it using your model—they're dinosaurs. They'll be sitting on their ass on the sofa in October watching the Boston Red Sox win the World Series."

That was a bold prediction considering that the Red Sox hadn't won a baseball championship since 1918. That's when the Red Sox sold the contract of the legendary Babe Ruth (often called the "Bambino") to the New York Yankees. Ever since then, fans have referred to the Red Sox's losing streak as the "Curse of the Bambino." If history was any indicator of future performance, the owner's prophetic statement was more wishful thinking than possibility.

Yet he was right. The year after following in Beane's footsteps, the Red Sox broke the curse and won the World Series. From 2004 to 2018, the baseball team won four titles altogether.

The owner was right about another thing—the sport radically changed. Soon, every team had begun to follow Oakland and the Red Sox. Teams abandoned the old way of baseball—based largely on recruiting players for their individual successes—and embraced the new approach of recruiting players based on whether they would contribute to the success of the overall team. The method Beane adopted is called "sabermetrics," which looks at a baseball team as an interconnected system instead of a collection of individual players.

This quantitative approach to assessing baseball players was made possible because of three things: cheaper computing power, grassroots data collection, and 20-plus years of conviction. (The very same things that have enabled the development of the capex strategy approach presented in this book.)

We're reminded of an observation by baseball legend Mickey Mantle when he said, "It's amazing how much you don't know about the game you've been playing your whole life." The same is true for capital expenditure.

Our approach to capital budgeting decision-making doesn't view whether a capex project is a good decision or a bad one. That's too simplistic a view, and companies lose substantial amounts of money with that perspective. We create an economic model of the company's entire production system and then rank *whole collections* of capex decisions against each other. Instead of asking whether the company should pursue a capex project, we embed the project in a larger series of capital allocation decisions and then ask, Does this chain of decisions make the system perform better or worse than another chain?

This counter-conventional approach has uncovered vast opportunities: no less than a 20% increase in company cash flow and, more than once, a 100% increase. Capex decisions are more than simply approving and prioritizing projects. A true capital allocation strategy transforms the core of the company, impacting every other facet of the organization.

Before sabermetrics, baseball teams focused on getting the best players. In a sense, owners and managers used analytical thinking to solve the problem of winning. They broke the team into its most basic components—player positions—and then tried to optimize the person who played that position. The assumption was that enough all-star players would result in a winning team.

Beane didn't know it at the time, but by embracing this new way of recruiting players, he embraced systems thinking. He didn't ask, How do we get better players? That fight came down to who had the biggest budget and paid the most to attract the best. Instead, Beane asked, How do we get more wins? He didn't need all-star players—he needed an all-star *team*.

After some data-crunching, baseball experts found the number one correlation between players' individual performance and their team's wins: their collective group's on-base percentage. Oakland could afford to run their own numbers since the price of computers and computing power had become so cheap by the late 1990s. The team found a number of players who had been overlooked and undervalued because recruiters were looking at them through the wrong lens.

In preparing to write this book, we discovered one of the most important figures in systems thinking. He also happens to be one of the most influential figures in manufacturing operations, supply chain management, and industrial engineering, among other fields: Dr. W. Edwards Deming, the "prophet of quality." His teachings at Toyota, Sony, Nissan, Boeing, AT&T, and others were the genesis of the Toyota Production System, Six Sigma, lean manufacturing, statistical process/quality control, and even agile software development. Unsurprisingly, we found that our economics-based approach to capital allocation developed over the past 25 years dovetails with his systems thinking-based approach to management, productivity, and performance.

Using our process, we've found that today's analytical approach to capex results in capital budgeting decisions driven by the needs and opportunities of individual parts of the production system. We often refer to this as "the tail wags the dog." Capital allocation should be driven by the existing capex needs and opportunities over an entire company, as seen from that portfolio perspective. It sounds like the same thing. It isn't. Moreover, capital allocation should be an intentional process of designing the company for the next 10 to 15 years. Today, however, companies are unintentionally and more randomly being designed by a piecemeal capex process. The company's future becomes wherever the individual needs of its production processes and assets take it.

Like Beane, the first step to overturning the old way is to settle on the right metric . . . because the metric companies use today hides those very capex opportunities they're looking for.

## DOES CAPEX EQUAL VALUE?

Different companies have different ways to measure the value of a capex project. Some use net present value (NPV) or an internal rate of return (IRR) while others may simply use payback periods or some mix thereof. Regardless of how it gauges performance, every company we've ever worked with or heard of uses metrics based on one common principle: the difference (or delta) between a production asset's cash flow with the capital expenditure and that asset's cash flow without it.

We've found that the most straightforward way to explain why cash flow deltas are misleading is to use a simplified illustration of a hypothetical company with three production sites. Let's say Quality Pulp Manufacturing, Inc. has three pulp mills. Its Baton Rouge, Louisiana, mill has been in operation for about 20 years. Like any mill, its cash flow is somewhat volatile from year to year as the market changes, as the price of wood climbs, and so on. However, with some simple math, we can normalize the mill's cash flow over the years. This gives us a good frame of reference; we can understand how the mill has performed over time. Quality Pulp assumes the mill will maintain its operations for the foreseeable future as it has over the past 20 years . When we graph its normalized cash flows over the last few years and project them into the future, it results in Figure 1.3.

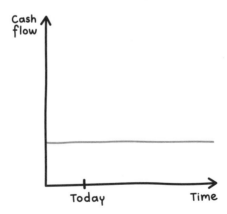

Of course, the executives at Quality Pulp expect that Baton Rouge will require a number of capexes over time. Machinery and equipment wear out, the market expects a certain level of quality, and so forth. In fact, the company has already made several such investments.

The manager sees that quality has become a real issue for the company's customers. No one at the corporate office is surprised when the mill manager submits a capex request. Between discounts, reruns, and losses to the competition, the mill's performance is down.

"But," the manager says, "with this capex, things will go back to normal."

Corporate has two options. One, they can deny the request, in which case the mill's cash flow will soon decline. Without any further intervention, the mill itself will eventually become obsolete. Obviously, that's not a viable option. So the company goes with option two and allocates a portion of the capital budget for this capex request. This will allow Baton Rouge's cash flow to continue as it has been.

Figure 1.4 graphs the cash flows of the two options. If corporate had chosen to deny the request, cash flow would have fallen (as depicted by the dotted line). Or corporate could make a one-time capital expenditure to maintain nominal cash flow. The difference between the two cash flows is called the delta. (As we'll see, this delta is the foundation of such conventional capex metrics as NPV, IRR, payback, and more. We also use NPV for calculations, but it's through a different lens.)

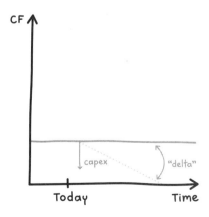

In our example, we assume all the data used and calculations made are correct and that all assumptions/predictions will come to pass. This resembles real life in that we've found companies rarely have a data quality issue. Most of the time, their analyses result in positive cash flow deltas. Faulty data or incorrect assumptions are not what leads to suboptimal capital allocation decisions.

> ## Data Is Not the Problem
>
> *In truth, it doesn't matter how good or bad the underlying data is. Today's approach to capex results in bad capex decisions regardless of data quality. The issue isn't one of assumptions but of a fundamentally flawed way of thinking.*

The number crunchers at Quality Pulp Manufacturing convert the capex cash flow delta into today's equivalent value and arrive at a net present value of $30. (This $30 could mean $30,000 or $30 million; these calculations scale to any size capex project.) The number crunchers also find that the project has a 24-month payback.

There's a known quality issue, a positive NPV, and a quick payback. To everyone involved, this looks like a good capex decision. Corporate approves and earmarks the funds in the coming year's capex budget.

Three months later, the manager of the Baton Rouge mill submits another capex request. The woodyard has an issue that's beginning to become a real cost problem. The company goes through the whole capex analysis process again. The result shows a positive cash flow delta with a solid NPV of $50 and a 30-month payback. Corporate approves the request.

This pattern continues over the next two years. The screens need to be replaced. An evaporator needs to be refurbished. A conveyer needs to be upgraded. Each time, corporate faces the stark choice: Do nothing and let cash flow fall or make the investment to maintain it? The NPV total of these projects is $200, representing the accumulated benefit from all capex projects.

If we were to graph those 10 projects from today's vantage point, it would look like Figure 1.5.

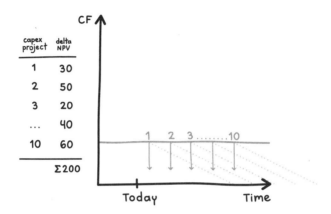

Without each subsequent capex invested, Baton Rouge's cash flow will fall. The site will eventually become obsolete. Quality Pulp must invest time and time again, not to improve the mill's cash flow, but to *restore and maintain its existing normalized cash flow*. None of these capexes fundamentally improves the mill's performance. Each one merely postpones the mill's obsolescence. As we said, after adding the NPVs of each request all together, we get $200. How does that number relate to the value of the site? Before answering that question let's look into the investment proposals of Quality Pulp's two other production sites.

## Capexes Don't Add Value . . . as a Rule

Most capex projects do not add value. Most investments, at best, maintain the value already promised in an earlier, often larger expansion capex project. If a company were to do a greenfield capex calculation, it might estimate its useful life to be 20 years. It would also estimate a flat figure for its earnings before interest, taxes, depreciation, and amortization (EBITDA). Will the greenfield reach that 20-year mark with a flat EBITDA without any capex projects? No. The company will continuously have to invest in this facility to achieve what it claims in the greenfield request. Everyone knows this. Those additional capex projects do not create new value. The value traditionally calculated is what's *rescued* from the original value promised before the site was built. The company will only add further value if it adds more capacity or makes another step-change decision that changes the trajectory of the facility's performance.

If you have a particular site, then the value of that site is determined by the future cash flow from the site, not by the NPVs of a capex plan.

Replacing the tires on an eight-year-old Volvo doesn't increase the car's value; the market still values it as an eight-year-old car. Likewise, replacing a piece of equipment of a 20-year-old mill doesn't change the site's value.

# THE FATAL FLAW OF
# CASH FLOW DELTAS

The scientific method dictates that to effectively compare two experiments, only one variable can change. Everything else must remain constant. In our example here, we're going to hold everything constant between Baton Rouge and the other two mills. The one variable will be the mills' normalized cash flows.

Quality Pulp has another mill in Cleveland, Ohio. It has run for 60 years. Although the company has approved most of its

required capexes, the mill simply can't compete against the industry average. Its normalized cash flow going forward is calculated to
be virtually zero. However, to maintain operations at an acceptable
quality, the company must continue to allocate part of its capital
budget for repairs and maintenance.

On the same day the Baton Rouge manager submits his first
capex request, the Cleveland manager submits an identical capex
request. Furthermore, all of its requested capexes are the exact
same as Baton Rouge's: same capex amounts, same cost savings,
same energy consumption improvements, same quality gains,
same safety and environmental compliance costs, same productivity gains, and so on. Logically, the differences between Cleveland's
normalized cash flows and its otherwise declining cash flows—
that is, the deltas—for the exact same projects will be the exact
same as in Baton Rouge. Therefore, Cleveland will have the same
NPV for its capex projects as Baton Rouge: $200.

If we were to graph these two mills' cash flows and capexes
together, we'd get Figure 1.6.

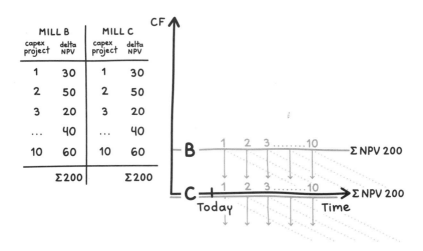

Before we examine the implications of this graph, let's add the
third mill in Albuquerque, New Mexico. The company built this
greenfield site just 10 years ago. Its state-of-the-art technology

makes the mill's performance a leader in the industry. Again, holding all factors but one constant results in identical cash flow deltas totaling $200. When we add Albuquerque to our graph, it looks like Figure 1.7.

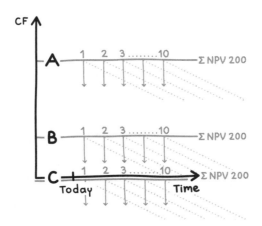

According to today's approach to capex, these three mills provide the same value from all of their capex projects. Their required capex needs have the exact same cash flow deltas. It doesn't seem to matter which capexes the company approves; their NPVs are identical. Yet Cleveland generates zero cash flow for the company and Albuquerque generates most of Quality Pulp's revenue. How can this be? And, again, how does the $200 in NPV relate to the value of the sites?

Looking at the graph in Figure 1.7, it should be clear. Delta NPVs on capex calculations have no mathematical relation to the value of a site or business. Absolutely none whatsoever. Yes, we've oversimplified this example, but this only puts the problem in stark contrast. From a capital budgeting process, all three of these sites are equally good investments because they measure performance *by differences in cash flows—not actual cash flow.*

From our experience, reality only serves to confuse the picture even more.

> *Cash flow deltas do not equal cash flow.*

# REALITY IS WORSE

A more accurate picture of how the capex requests for these three particular facilities would show up in the standard capital allocation process would look something like the graph in Figure 1.8.

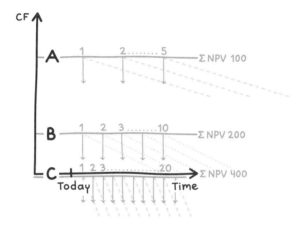

In a 60-year-old mill like Cleveland, cash flows will decline much more quickly without an intervening capex than in a much younger mill like Albuquerque. That means the gap between fixing the problem versus not (i.e., the cash flow delta) will be much wider in Cleveland than in Albuquerque. If Cleveland implements the quality-enhancing capex project, the mill might save $10 in annual removed rebates and regained volumes. That sounds impressive, but it's only because the company is replacing a piece of equipment from the 1980s with its cutting-edge equivalent. That is, the calculation has a poor starting point; the mill was already in a poor position to begin with. If Albuquerque were to upgrade the same 10-year-old piece of equipment, the mill might only save $5 because it was in a rather good position to begin with.

Cleveland's capex projects look as impressive as they do only because the mill is so old. Since Quality Pulp fixes a large problem every time it does something there, the company closes the gap from a currently poor situation to bring that piece of equipment up to state of the art. These types of sites create larger cash flow deltas, resulting in higher NPVs. The greater the delta, the quicker the payback. That's how the flawed math works. But again, none of these capex investments will improve the site's overall cash flow—at least, not at any substantial level. Value has not been created, only rescued. Cleveland's capexes simply maintain its zero cash flow. Everything else in Cleveland (probably 99% of the asset's replacement value) will continue to age.

> *The older the asset, the higher the capex NPV and the shorter the payback. The effectiveness of the "medicine" (i.e., the capex) is a function of age and disease—not how fundamentally healthy the asset is from an actual cash flow perspective.*

Furthermore, because Cleveland is an aging mill, it will have more capex needs than Baton Rouge and certainly more than Albuquerque. There are more liability issues, more replacements due to age and quality needs, and more safety and environmental regulations the mill is behind on. The more capex needs it has, the higher the site's sum of its capex projects' NPVs. Going by the larger deltas and the greater number of capexes needed, Cleveland's capex NPVs could add up to something more like $400—despite creating no value for Quality Pulp's shareholders.*

---

* Not all companies approach this situation the same way. Some companies do not make delta calculations on "forced" capexes (such as adhering to safety regulations, pure replacements due to age, etc.). But the endgame is the same. It is still a piecemeal decision-making process without the strategic capex calculation behind it.

This amount does not in any way reflect reality, of course. Each capex request is calculated the same way, one by one in isolation . . . which means the same cash flow is now paying off two capex projects. You can see in Figure 1.8 how the areas of the cash flow deltas overlap. Each capex project uses the same cash flows to justify its value. This is the equivalent of remortgaging a home in a second bank and then a third.

With every new capex request, the calculations ignore the "debt" from the previously requested capex projects. The same revenue stream must now pay for two capex projects, despite the fact neither increased cash flow. The payback periods for the first and second projects have to be updated. If both projects had a payback period of two years and the mill's cash flow stream had to be evenly divided between them. That would mean the first project's "debt" would take longer than two years to pay off. The second project couldn't be paid back in two years if half the cash went to cover the first project. With half the cash flow, it would take twice as long.

> *The worst-performing sites have the best-looking capex projects.*
> *You can always find a "good" capex in a bad mill.*

Contrast that to Albuquerque. That site is only 10 years old. At that age, it operates at near its life cycle's peak performance. The gap between its post-capex cash flows versus no capex cash flows is fairly small. It has few safety and environmental issues. There are fewer benefits to upgrading its equipment and machines since most of the mill is still state of the art. There may be a few opportunities, but these capexes can never compete with the short payback projects from Cleveland and Baton Rouge. With smaller deltas, the sum of Albuquerque's capex delta NPVs is much less. A star performer like Albuquerque would probably have a capex total of NPVs closer to $100.

Even though Cleveland is all but obsolete, the conventional approach to capex says it's the best investment. Even though Albuquerque's revenues are practically propping up the company, the conventional approach says to disregard it completely. Altogether, Quality Pulp Manufacturing's capex plans for each mill are inversely correlated with each mill's value. The better a site performs, the fewer capexes it needs; the worse a site performs, the more capexes there are and, therefore, the higher the value of its capex plan. The company's approach to capex magnifies Cleveland's "opportunities" and minimizes Albuquerque's needs and contributions.

According to the company's capex process, Quality Pulp should invest the lion's share of its capex budget in Cleveland . . . so that the mill can continue to generate no cash flow. Its capex process does not highlight this zero cash flow reality, however, because it's difficult to see it when viewing capital allocation decisions project by project instead of as an interconnected system. In truth, the only way for a capex project to create value in Cleveland would probably be a complete rebuild of the mill or adding significant capacity, but that project would have a long payback and couldn't compete with smaller, incremental capexes with shorter paybacks. Conversely, the company's capex process says Quality Pulp should invest the least in Albuquerque, despite it being the best-performing site and generating most of the company's cash flow.

So far, we have talked about one aspect of cash flow: the valuation aspect. When a company is financially challenged, a second aspect of cash flow becomes important: the liquidity aspect. Seeking to maintain or improve liquidity, during these times company executives prioritize capex projects with even shorter paybacks. A site like Cleveland looks like the go-to mill for capex projects since this site will "rescue" the company in these rough times. Money will come back quicker if capex is spent in Cleveland, and this can be used to repay loans. A site like Albuquerque is even further neglected.

The term "payback" itself is misleading, to say the least. It is not about payback. In truth, the company will never recover its investments in Cleveland even if all assumptions come into play. All capex projects' NPVs and short paybacks are actually realized from a postcompletion review point of view, but the company will never see any money come back. How can it with a site that generates no cash flow? That value is simply gone; there is no payback in terms of money. The company will never recoup its capital invested, much less ever see Cleveland contribute much (if anything) to overall company cash flow.

> If you were to take all the promises of each capex project in this mill implemented over the last 10 years and put them together, we would have an EBITDA margin of over 100%.
> —Project team member

At some point, the bill comes due. The amount of capexes required to keep the site in operation exceeds the site's overall cash flow. When we review our clients' production sites, we almost always find at least one site projected to have virtually zero cash flow in the near future. We've seen a vast number of sites where the capexes required, in combination with a declining EBITDA margin, resulted in a negative net cash flow.

This is how poor companies go bankrupt. They spend their last dimes on their worst assets because that's where they believe they will get money back the fastest. The more quickly they recoup their investment, the more quickly they can pay off debt and/or make a capital investment somewhere else. The faster payback, the faster cash flow. At least, that's what they think.

*Capex decisions based on cash flow deltas destroy shareholder value.*

As we stated, our example here assumes the data and calculations are 100% correct. Reality is more complicated, but that only obscures the true picture. The complexity of the real world doesn't change the fundamental fact that cash flow deltas direct more resources to underperforming assets and divert more resources away from high-performing ones.

The problem is that cash flow deltas are relative. A cash flow delta doesn't share a fixed reference point with other deltas; it uses itself as its reference. The delta measures the difference between cash flow with capex and cash flow without capex. This means that an effective cash flow delta will practically *always* return a positive delta *even for an asset with a negative cash flow.* That's how the math works.

Some companies avoid the worst decisions by additionally relying on some "gut feelings" when making decisions. In our view, this isn't any worse than following today's capex process when looking at a portfolio of perhaps one or two sites. But for companies with multiple sites (certainly more than three), gut feelings cannot be relied on. The C-suite must follow a process, if for no other reason than governance and accountability.

Other companies look at their sites' future cash flows—maybe categorizing the sites into quartiles 1–4 or divisions A, B, or C—and allow that to influence the capex budgeting process. Compared to blindly following today's capex process, that is slightly better. But it's still putting duct tape on the capex process. It does not solve the major problem: companies don't have an effective way to see their production portfolios as a system of cash flows, precluding them from seeing how to best allocate their capital. They believe they do, but after working with scores of capital-intensive multinational companies, we've found they all use a similarly flawed perspective.

Some companies categorize their divisions into A, B, and C, where A is a division in a growing market, C is in a declining market, and B is in the middle. Within each division you might find A, B, and C sites. So you can have a C site in an A division, and an A site in a C division. While categorization probably brings some good discussions on performance, it is of little actual help when allocating capex. Especially since some companies will underinvest in their C divisions' A sites (because of the categorization), which might have the best opportunities of them all. To categorize is not a plan and companies cannot create a plan from it. The wiser way comes from establishing a systemwide calculated capex strategy.

> *You'll have a positive cash flow delta even with a negative cash flow asset.*

To complicate matters even further, no one can correctly identify a company's all-star performers like Albuquerque (its "A sites") from its middling "B sites" like Baton Rouge nor its financial liabilities like Cleveland (a.k.a. its "C sites") by analyzing each in isolation. Not even we can correctly identify such all-stars at the beginning of a client engagement.

By definition, you cannot assess the value of a system's component in isolation. To find what it's worth to the system, you have to measure the system's output with and then without the component. To find Cleveland's (or any other site's) value, Quality Pulp would have to look at its portfolio's cash flow today, then run an economic simulation of how the portfolio would run in its absence. The difference between those two cash flows is the true measure of Cleveland's worth to Quality Pulp's production system. The EBITDA, return on capital employed (ROCE), or even cash flow (when viewed in isolation) from an individual site is irrelevant to understanding its contribution to the overall production system.

> *No one can see an asset's value without a holistic view of the larger production system.*

# 2

# FROM ISOLATED PROJECTS TO INTEGRATED SYSTEMS

At the outbreak of the Covid-19 pandemic in 2020, our native Sweden took a quite different approach than most countries. While much of Europe, North America, and elsewhere essentially told their citizens (children and adults alike) to shelter in place, Swedes were carrying on with their lives very much as normal. Yes, there were some recommendations, though many were voluntary, and a few restrictions. But by and large, life went on as it had been. Setting aside the question of which approach is better, let's instead ask: Why would a developed economy take such a radically different approach than its peers?

It's a matter of perspective. In other countries, national governments immediately put epidemiologists in charge of their pandemic response. It makes logical sense. Those experts focused on the pressing problem of mitigating Covid-19's spread; that was what they'd been tasked with. In Sweden, however, the entities with the power over public health care are responsible not just for providing health care but also for ensuring a high overall quality of life. The powers that be weighed the costs of a national lockdown, including disrupted education, children losing playmates and interaction, social anxiety, depression, individual costs, and more, and they then made a different decision.

Other nations took an analytical approach: People are dying from Covid-19—how do we stop it from spreading?

Sweden took a systems approach: People are dying from Covid-19—how would different responses affect overall quality of life?

If the goal was to minimize Covid-related deaths, perhaps Sweden fared worse than it otherwise would have. If the goal was to maintain a high quality of life and health care (including considering Covid-related deaths), perhaps Sweden fared better than other countries. Again, which approach is better is subjective: it depends on how a country defines "better."

Perspective dictates perception.

## THE EFFICIENCY PARADOX

In Chapter 1, we mentioned the efficiency paradox. To see it in effect, consider the fatal case of GM's ignition switch that came to light in 2014. In some vehicles, the faulty part suddenly shut off the engine while driving. While that would be dangerous enough on its own, another factor made it even worse—the airbags wouldn't deploy when the engine was off.

Imagine speeding down the interstate with cruise control set at 70 mph. Out of nowhere, the engine shuts off—which automatically turns off power steering and power brakes. On top of the natural panic, the driver now has to wrestle with steering and braking problems they've never encountered. When the car inevitably veers into another lane, over the median, or into the concrete divider and crashes—still traveling the same speed—none of the airbags work.

While it sounds like something out of a horror movie, this was the reality for hundreds of drivers. In 2014, GM recalled 800,000 vehicles and then 1.5 million. Soon recalls had been issued for more than six million vehicles. By the end, nearly 30 million cars were recalled worldwide. The official standing death toll is 124 people—all because of an electrical switch that cost less than a dollar.

What does this have to do with capital expenditure?

Perhaps the title of this *Harvard Business Review* article captures it best: "Optimizing Each Part of a Firm Doesn't Optimize the Whole Firm." Various GM engineers, attorneys, and managers had known about the problem since 2005, almost a full decade before the first recall. Investigating on behalf of Congress, US Attorney Anton Valukas "found that GM didn't fix its ignition-switch issues quickly or correctly because the company's many departments and employees literally weren't communicating with one another."[*] While engineers in one department looked into the problem of cars stalling, engineers in another department designed airbags that would not deploy unless the engine was running. Each department sought to optimize its subsystem or subcomponent of responsibility, independent of how it interacted with others'. They each focused on a part of the car without looking at the whole. The HBR article said, "When we see an operation as a set of isolated metrics to optimize, we can lose our sense of context and decrease overall performance—an efficiency paradox."[†]

If GM had taken the macro view instead of the micro, maybe those 124 people would have lived out their natural lives. Humanity aside, taking the wider view would have certainly avoided the $600 million in victim compensation claims as well as the forfeiture of $900 million to the US government.

Likewise, the perspective of the mill manager at Cleveland from Chapter 1 is necessarily a limited one. He has been tasked

---

[*] Satell, G., 2016. "Optimizing Each Part of a Firm Doesn't Optimize the Whole Firm." [online] *Harvard Business Review.* https://hbr.org/2016/01/optimizing-each -part-of-a-firm-doesnt-optimize-the-whole-firm

[†] Ibid.

with maintaining the site's operations. He is necessarily and appropriately focused on keeping things as they are. His job is to do what's best for his site, to keep it running, not what's best for the company. The overall performance, effectiveness, and competitiveness of Quality Pulp Manufacturing as a company isn't part of his perspective. That's not his job.

> *Site managers pursue capex projects to sustain operations—not to maximize shareholder value.*

When the mill manager submits a capex request, corporate doesn't ask, "Is this the best use of the company's capital?" In fact, the manager doesn't even try to maximize his own mill's long-term cash flow. As an example, it is unusual that a site manager proposes to shut the site, even if that obviously is the best choice from a cash flow point of view. He submits capex proposals that keep Cleveland in production. To keep customers happy and to return an EBITDA margin—that's his job.

Instead, the question is more along the lines of, Is this capex necessary to maintain Cleveland's operations? or, Will this opportunity deliver a good payback? While unintentional, this results in a bottom-up approach to capex. Capital budgeting is driven by the needs and opportunities of individual sites instead of a coordinated, top-down strategy. The system's effectiveness should be the priority—not the needs and opportunities of the system's components.

This bottom-up perspective forces a tactical approach: What projects do we need or want to spend money on? It precludes a strategic perspective: How should we allocate our capital throughout our portfolio of production sites to maximize company cash flow? Those questions are completely different and their answers result in completely different capital allocation decisions.

*Today's companies have a collection of capex projects— not a capex strategy.*

## INDIVIDUAL PERFORMANCE VERSUS INDUSTRY AVERAGE

In baseball, the general manager (GM) is in charge of the macro-level decisions. In Billy Beane's case, the decision was to recruit baseball players based on analytics instead of box scores and intuition. The team manager is in charge of the tactical-level decisions. During a game, from moment to moment this manager evaluates which players would best fill what position.

In the movie, Beane's antagonist is his manager, Art Howe. Where Beane sees an all-star team, Howe sees an "island of misfit toys." He refuses to play the team Beane's way. Instead of arguing with him, Beane trades some of Howe's favored players to other teams. Howe has little choice but to play the team like Beane wants. The manager isn't really to blame. His job is to make the most with what he has.

The job of site managers isn't to maximize company cash flow. When they were "handed the keys," so to speak, they were essentially told, Keep it in good shape. Keep it safely running. Maintain current levels of quality and keep the customers happy. Deliver an EBITDA. So, that's what they do. That's what their capex requests center around.

At the company's annual capital budgeting meeting, these types of projects are nearly all the capex projects the executive decision makers have to review: upgrading safety equipment, environmental compliance, rebuilding a major component, and so on. In addition to this, the executives might also consider a handful of strategic initiatives, such as building a greenfield, converting a production line to manufacture a specialty product, or increasing capacity at a site. But compared to the local sites' needs to maintain the facilities, these other capex opportunities are few and far between.

Over time, the capex improvements to a production asset add up. An asset is typically more efficient later in its life cycle than it is at the beginning. Continuous improvements result in speedups, automation, improved workflows, reduced waste, lower headcounts, and so forth. Whatever the case, it comes down to using fewer resources to make more and/or better products. This is true not only for individual machines, but for entire production sites as well.

Despite these improvements, a production site can never keep up with the industry's rate of technological advance. Even if every part of 60-year-old Cleveland was replaced, upgraded, or refurbished, it still couldn't match the superior workflows, scale, and layout of Albuquerque. Even though Cleveland is more efficient than it was when originally built, it simply cannot keep pace with greenfield sites or even existing sites like Baton Rouge. Cleveland's competitiveness may improve over time, but it cannot keep up with the industry's average competitiveness rate. The gap between its performance and the overall industry's will widen until it's too far to bridge. Visually, that might look like Figure 2.1.

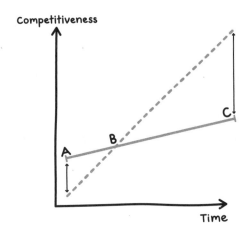

At the beginning of a production asset's life cycle (point A), it has a competitive advantage over the industry's collective average performance (the dotted line). When Cleveland was first built, it used best practices and the most advanced technology commercially available. Even though it improved over time (indicated by the slight upward slope of the solid line), the change isn't fast enough to maintain its advantage. Perhaps 15 or 20 years later, the two lines intersect (point B). Then, the site is an average-performing asset on par with its peers, perhaps where Baton Rouge is today. Over the years, the industry continues to outpace the mill's performance until the gap (at point C) is too great to overcome. Like every life cycle, a production asset must have an end.

Even if Quality Pulp decided to make a major investment and replace 10% of Cleveland's assets, it would take one to three years from decision to turnkey operation. During that time, the other 90% of the mill would age another three years. At best, the net effect would be that Cleveland doesn't become even *less* competitive than the industry average. That is, it wouldn't close the gap—the gap just wouldn't get worse, at least for those three years. The company can't practically or economically continue replacing 10% of the mill every three years. As such, the gap will continue to grow. As the mill becomes less competitive, its cash flow margins will continue to decline until it reaches the stage of our example: generating zero net cash flow.

## CAPEX TODAY MISALLOCATES RESOURCES

What if we extended our example? What if instead of 3 mills, Quality Pulp Manufacturing had a portfolio of 10? For simplicity's sake, let's assume that all of them make more or less the same product for more or less the same market. Let's also assume that, on average, this collection of pulp mills follows the industry average and has been built at a pace reflecting the industry average. Therefore, the company is average for its industry.

By definition, half of any given industry's capacity comes from assets operating above the industry's average competitiveness rate. The other half is, of course, produced by the below-average assets. It's not unlikely that it would have two more mills like Albuquerque, operating at above-average competitiveness. The three of these super-efficient mills together would probably generate at least half of the company's production. As we said earlier, we call these "A sites."

The other seven mills would therefore generate the other half of Quality Pulp's production volume. Cleveland, however, is getting dangerously close to becoming a financial liability. Earlier, we named it the company's C site. Let's call Baton Rouge and the remaining five production sites the company's B sites. The competitiveness of these would range from right at the industry average to barely better than Cleveland.

If we graphed all 10 sites according to their technical age/competitiveness, it would look like Figure 2.2.*

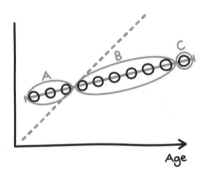

At the very end of a site's life cycle, it usually becomes apparent that it will soon have to be shut down. There is not yet a closure

---

* The academically inclined reader may notice that as we change the x axis from time to age the entire graph should rotate downward, making the dashed line flat, parallel to the x axis and the solid curve would be declining.

decision; it's just apparent that it will be closed in the next three to five years. Recognizing this, companies are reluctant to allocate much of the capex budget . . . even if the capex projects look good on paper. This is when executives start deviating from normal capex procedure, ignoring the data because they recognize what's going to happen in reality. After working with dozens of clients and several hundreds of sites, we find companies typically spend 3–5% of their annual capex budget on obvious C sites—typically just enough to prolong their inevitable demise and to keep operations safely running.

It's easy to understand why most companies don't heavily invest in their A sites. Those facilities' capex "needs" are minimal. There are few quality, safety, and environmental issues. A capex investment would only marginally improve productivity, but not enough to make a sizable impact so that it could compete with paybacks from B and C sites. From our experience, most companies spend something like 20%, sometimes 25%, of their capex budgets on their A sites (again, these generate half of their production volume).

The remaining 75% of the capex budget goes to the company's B sites. This is a large category with six sites. Anything from a well-performing site (those B sites toward the left of the competitiveness curve), to the one marginally better than the C site. These are often complex sites, sometimes with two or three pieces of major equipment in various states of relative competitiveness (versus the more homogenous mix of asset ages at A sites), and they have building issues. The layout is often not optimal.

For instance, we remember once being given a tour in a B site. We were very well acquainted with the industry and knew the production process well. Every time a door into another part of the site was opened, there was a surprise waiting for us. The finished goods area was right after raw material intake. Then came the energy island, then converting, and so on. It was as if the site had been designed helter-skelter, with no rhyme or reason for production flows. Unfortunately, this is all too common. In these types of sites, there are also often environmental and safety issues requiring investment. B sites' requests are generally deemed worthwhile. The fact that two-thirds of sites within a company receive about three-quarters of the capex budget isn't a shock to anyone.

Table 2.1 summarizes this capex budget spread.

**Table 2.1**

| Site Category | A | B | C |
|---|---|---|---|
| Annual Capex Invested | 20% | 75% | 5% |

We've seen this spread again and again. Industries from agriculture to mining to consumer goods on all continents gravitate into this capex split. Since virtually all manufacturing companies use virtually the same capex process, this makes sense. As we said, aside from an obvious impending closure like Cleveland, companies rarely categorize their sites in a useful way, in no small part because they can't sort their star performers from the middling production sites without a systems-thinking tool. The ones we have seen who try to categorize have failed. They have made incorrect categorizations and draw the wrong conclusions from the categorization. We only find this capex allocation spread ourselves after running a capex strategy model and determining individual sites' contribution to the company's overall cash flow. Categorizations cannot be made based on cost curves, profitability, margins, capex project opportunities, or even the facility's cash flow.

We find that while our clients' A sites produce about half of the production volume, they will generate something close to 80% of cash flow in the next 5–10 years, even after deducting for the sites' capex investments. This makes sense. Sites like Albuquerque are the most competitive, have the highest margins, and require the least amount of capexes.

In fact, we've even seen cases where these A assets generate more than 100% of company cash flow—in one case, 300% of future cash flows. (Think about how the math works out for that company's collective mill portfolio to altogether total 100%. The A sites were not only paying for themselves but paying for the B and C sites, too.)

As we said, if Quality Pulp is lucky, Cleveland will continue to generate zero cash flow. Baton Rouge and the rest of the B sites contribute the remaining 20% of company cash flow (again, after having received 75% of the capital). When we update Table 2.1, we see the following:

| Site Category | A | B | C |
|---|---|---|---|
| Annual Capex Invested | 20% | 75% | 5% |
| Cash Flow After Capexes | 80% | 20% | 0% |

Already we can see a disparity emerging. The typical company allocates an inordinate proportion of its capex budget to sites that generate a fraction of its total cash flow. That's not to mention investing capex dollars into a site that provides no cash flow whatsoever. Only a fraction of the capex budget goes to the sites that are the real economic engines of the company—the powerhouses that keep pouring money into the company's coffers.

Lastly, we look at how management allocates time among these three site categories. We ask our clients to identify their 100 key people in human resources, engineering, controlling, market, manufacturing, procurement, project management, and so forth. Then we ask, "How much attention do you collectively spend on each category? Exclude budget meetings, report reviews, and so on. Focus solely on true quality time, including analysis, the discussions on evaluating the current state of the asset, estimating closure costs, considering whether to make a substantial capital investment, the results of each option, and more. How much time from your top 100 people goes into each category?"

When pushed to put pen to paper, executives come to realize that they have spent far more time figuring out what to do with their "problem child" than they have their star production assets. By these managers' own admission, C sites get an astounding 30%

of their time. These are the sites that are not worth anything, from a cash flow point of view. The 30% comes mostly from time spent trying to "fix" the site but also on evaluating closure costs, on discussions about reassigning production from elsewhere to keep the site running, and on the decisions to be made when it finally comes time to execute the closure.

A client of ours dragged a closure decision on for years. At one point, executive management had finally made the choice to close it for good. A senior VP got on the corporate jet and flew to the other side of the country. When he landed and could get cell phone coverage again, he found he had a voicemail waiting for him from the corporate office: "We got a large order. Come back." He turned around, boarded the jet, refueled, and flew home. Meanwhile, the site kept operating, consuming resources while generating zero net cash flow. The site is closed now.

Because A sites have few problems, they don't require much attention. In fact, an ex-manager at one A site told us he hadn't heard from corporate for the five years he had managed the mill. The site was relatively new and operations were running smoothly. Since the site didn't have any fires to put out, corporate turned its attention elsewhere. All in all, we find companies typically spend, at most, 5% of their time with sites like this one. The remaining 65% of their productive time goes toward their B sites.

Further building out Table 2.1 gives us:

| Site Category | A | B | C |
|---|---|---|---|
| Annual Capex Invested | 20% | 75% | 5% |
| Cash Flow After Capexes | 80% | 20% | 0% |
| Management Attention | 5% | 65% | 30% |

Sites with no cash flow (if not negative cash flow) get nearly one-third of one of the company's most valuable resource: management attention. Sites that contribute only a fifth of net cash flow take up two-thirds of management's time. The economic engines that power the whole company barely get two-and-a-half weeks of the top resources' attention over the course of a year.

How much is a company's top 100 employees' time and attention worth? Does it make sense to spend almost a third of those resources dedicated to an aging production asset? Does it make sense that they spend 95% of their time on middling assets that generate only 20% of total company cash flow? Does it make sense for the manager of a category A site—generating the lion's share of the business—to go five years without hearing from the executive team? Lastly, is it sustainable for a company to devote the least resources to its best performing assets?

Table 2.1 isn't theoretical. It summarizes information from scores of clients across dozens of industries managing hundreds of industrial sites. This isn't intentional on the part of the companies' leadership. Few realize they do this. Some initially outright deny this is the case at all. Over 25 years of analyzing our clients' data, however, we've found this holds true.

Companies' executives often believe they have correctly identified and sorted their A, B, and C sites. They may have, but without a systems-thinking approach, they're comparing sites to each other just like they compare capex projects to each other. Sites' categorization cannot be effectively identified by anyone without creating an economic model that encompasses system cash flows and then running economic projections with and without each site. At best, the way companies sort their production sites today may help them avoid the worst capital allocation mistakes tomorrow.

But even if a company were able to correctly identify which sites were which, it still wouldn't provide an effective capex strategy. The two of us cannot make blanket statements such as, "Always run your C sites for cash," or, "Only invest what's necessary in

B sites." Our message is far worse: identifying your best and worst mills provides little help in reaching a capex strategy that maximizes operating cash flow.

Simply put: leadership is flying blind.

## Warren Buffett's Worst Investment

In an interview on CNBC, the fabled "Oracle of Omaha," the legendary investor Warren Buffett, said the worst stock he ever bought was . . . Berkshire Hathaway. Well, he actually described it as the "dumbest" investment he'd ever made. Why would he say such a thing when his company name is synonymous with his own?

He first invested in Berkshire Hathaway in 1962 when it was still a textile company, albeit a failing one. Thinking to make a profit as the US textile industry consolidated, he bet big. Two years later, however, the CEO there tried to underhandedly force the investor to pay an eighth of a point more for company stock. As revenge, Buffett bought the entire company outright, fired the CEO, and hired another. He then spent the next two decades largely propping up the company mostly out of spite. After all, if he closed the company, then the former CEO would "win," right? The Oracle estimates his business empire would be twice its size if he hadn't wasted so much time and money keeping a dying company on life support.

At the time of the interview, Berkshire Hathaway was worth $200 billion.

In 1975, Buffett bought another failing company, Waumbec Textile, which had just one mill. Years later, he would write, "The purchase price was a bargain based on the assets we received and the projected synergies with

Berkshire's existing textile business."* Soon after buying Waumbec, he was forced to close the mill, admitting the acquisition was a "terrible" decision.

This disproportionate investment of capex dollars and management attention comes from leadership often miscategorizing production sites. Going by the conventional measures of mill performance skews leadership's perspective. Judging from its return on capital employed (ROCE), a C site might appear like a B site. We even had one client who saw its star performer as the dog of the group.

At most, half of the clients we work with even have A sites operating at above-average competitiveness in their industries. Half of the remaining companies we've seen have only B and C sites; they don't have any all-star players. They usually don't recognize their C sites until one to two years before they're forced to close them. Even for the companies that have A sites, they often see them as middling production sites like Baton Rouge because the A sites show such a poor ROCE. As a result, leadership continues to allocate time and company resources to their least-performing assets and all but ignore their best.

## Taking the Long View

The CFO of forestry company SCA, Toby Lawton, had this to say:

> The trick to an effective capital asset strategy is identifying early where you're going to invest for the long

---

* 2014 Annual Shareholder Report. Omaha, NE: Berkshire Hathaway. 2014.

term, what is a cash cow, and which site where you're not going to invest over the bare minimum you have to. For the latter, it's knowing that in five years, or whatever the case might be, that the site is going to reach the end of its life and need to be shuttered. There are very few management teams who take that kind of strategic view 5 to 10 years ahead of time.

Usually, this type of site gets to a place where everyone is trying to save it. They do whatever it takes to keep it going. But eventually, they reach a point where there's simply no question; they know it must be closed. Unfortunately, this comes just after making substantial capital investments in the previous year or two trying to save it. In the end, all that money is wasted on what was a foregone conclusion to begin with.

This is a recipe for disaster if ever there was one. Unfortunately for shareholders, these impending disasters are slow-moving and hard to see. Without the proper lens, leaders blame company performance on poor pricing, rising costs, slow demand growth, and other such factors—systemic factors that all of their peers face as well. Companies do not go bad because the prices of their products are not going up as fast as the company hoped. Companies do not go bad because costs go up faster than expected or demand was weak. That would be like saying you lost a sailing race because you had the wind blowing in your face. Everybody faces the same systemic challenges. Conditions do not create poor companies or even a poor industry.

Why do some succeed where others end up in disaster? It is not that some companies are luckier with pricing or were dealt a better economic hand. It comes from superior capital allocation decisions; it's how leadership reacts to those conditions. Poor companies result from poor capital allocation and end up with poor competitiveness and cash flow. Companies allocate resources to assets not creating value and starve those that are.

> *We once presented to the board of a large European agriculture cooperative. At one point, we noticed that the directors began to nervously fidget in their chairs. We had just told them plenty of companies invest heavily in an aging mill only to find themselves having to close it down three or four years later. Unbeknownst to us, that exact scenario had played out in the company just the year before. They were still quite embarrassed by the experience. They felt that they had somehow been tricked or misled—despite all their capex calculations being entirely correct.*
>
> *Doubt. Regret. Confusion.*
>
> *These should not be the thoughts and feelings someone has when making multimillion-dollar decisions—decisions that may determine the fate of decision makers' careers, much less the fate of the company itself.*

## WHY PROFITABILITY MEASURES DON'T MATTER IN CAPITAL ALLOCATION DECISIONS

Past performance—as well as current—is relevant to making effective capital allocation decisions. More than relevant; it's vital for understanding where to best invest. This is because in industrial companies, capital assets need to be continually reinvested in, year after and year. Over a period of time, the entire asset base will eventually have to be completely rebuilt or abandoned. Capital allocation decisions should include historic performance in order to help understand the future potential. The problem is that companies don't have any sensible backward-looking measures that can inform forward-looking capital allocation decisions. That does not stop companies from using irrelevant profitability measures instead.

There are three prevailing myths that are part and parcel of how capex analyses and profitability measures are carried out today. The following counterintuitive statements—which fly in the face of conventional capex as it's currently practiced—shed light on these myths and their origins:

1. P&L and balance sheet measures such as . . .
   • Return on capital employed (ROCE)
   • Return on operating capital (ROOC)
   • Return on equity (ROE)
   • Economic value added (EVA)

   . . . are irrelevant to effective capital allocation decisions. They are influenced far more strongly by age than they are by actual performance and competitiveness. They skew and misconstrue the underlying asset's profitability.

2. Continually investing at a certain IRR for your capexes does not result in an equal EBITDA margin nor ROCE. That is, investing in capex projects with an IRR of 20% will not return an EBITDA margin of 20% nor a ROCE of 20%.* The calculations measure fundamentally different things. It's like seeing a drink on the shelf that's 40% alcohol and expecting a 40% discount at the cash register. The two percentages have nothing to do with each other.

---

* This is perhaps most easily understood by looking at Chapter 1's graphs for the A, B, and C mills.

3. Companies shouldn't make capital investments to improve their profitability. Instead, they should make capital investments to improve their long-term accumulated cash flow.

There are plenty of people who are part of the capital allocation process who don't understand why today's backward-looking performance measures cannot be used for forward-looking analyses.

## 1. P&L and Balance Sheet–Based Measures Are Irrelevant

CEOs, analysts, bankers, and other experts use ROCE and other such profit and loss (P&L) statement– and balance sheet–based measures to communicate a company's profitability. But in regard to capital allocation decisions, what are profitability measures there for in the first place? Why do we need them? The experts use them as proxies for measuring performance and assessing competitiveness. The underlying assumption is that if a profitability measure indicates the company is profitable than it means the company performs well and is competitive in the market, and that should provide the capital allocation process with vital input.

Again, that's the assumption.

If Quality Pulp's cost of capital is 10% and it averages 13% profitability over the years, then it is clearly competitive. That is, it financially performs 30% better than its cost of capital. This indicates the company performs well. Quality Pulp could have only achieved this by adding positive NPVs when building its business. That happens when you are better than the average competitor. (That explanation is a bit simplified but generally valid.) From an investment point of view, the company looks like an attractive investment: its management is able to multiply the dollars invested into it. Perhaps the company should even look into growing.

If Quality Pulp's profitability measure were instead 6%, then it underperformed. This indicates the business isn't competitive and is a substandard player in the market. Instead of trying to expand its business, in this case Quality Pulp would probably need to fix the company first.

If its profitability measure were a dismal 3%, that would indicate the company is not at all competitive. The managers of Quality Pulp should probably focus on exiting the business entirely or completely rebuilding its asset base (e.g., building greenfields and brownfield sites).

Companies need to have discussions around leadership's ability to profitably manage capital and how effective capital allocation decisions are. Such conversations necessitate fact-based profitability figures and performance measures as part of the discussion. Unfortunately, there are no such measures today. The profitability of the company is measured one way; how well its capital assets perform is something entirely different.

We've had some financial analysts argue that, although there are errors when using profitability measures to evaluate asset performance, these errors cancel out at the aggregate company or group level. (As one person put it, "Oh, it'll all come out in the wash.") We've been patiently waiting for them to show us how that works mathematically for, oh, a couple of decades now. It's an assumption, and we can show why it's an incorrect one.

Let's look at the EBITDA margin of Quality Pulp's mill in Cleveland. While the margin is volatile from year to year, we can use some simple mathematical tools to normalize it. Figure 2.3 shows its life cycle from being a greenfield 60 years ago to its performance today.

As is normally the case for greenfield sites, Cleveland's EBITDA margin was quite poor in its first year of operations. Parts of the site were still under construction, workflows were still being established, much of the production could not be sold, and so on. However, its margin quickly rose after that. At year five, its EBITDA margin peaked. Again, this makes intuitive sense: the five-year mark is usually a manufacturing site's sweet spot. Its performance is optimal and its technology and design put it best in class in its industry.

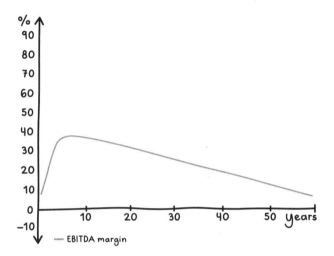

After its peak, however, Cleveland's EBITDA margin began to slowly decline as its assets began to age and as competitors built newer sites with even better material flows and more advanced technology. The mill simply can't maintain its competitive edge against such developments forever.

This decline came to pass despite Quality Pulp's continual capital expenditures in the Cleveland mill. In fact, the decline looks as it does precisely because of those capex investments. Otherwise, the margin would have declined much more quickly.

With the EBITDA margin normalized, it's easy to see this trend. At year 60, the mill's competitiveness has declined to nearly zero. In reality, the margin spikes and drops every year. People working at one site for 20 years may never notice the overall downward trend of that volatility.

Figure 2.4 overlays our graph of Cleveland's EBITDA margins over 60 years with a balance sheet measure like ROCE. ROCE is a mathematical consequence of the EBITDA and the capexes made, so we can calculate the ROCE over the life cycle with what we have.

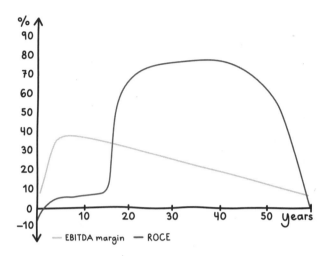

Cleveland's ROCE tells a quite different story. If—and we stress *if*—ROCE measured asset performance, then Cleveland wasn't competitive at all for its first 15 years of operations. Somehow, this multimillion dollar, state-of-the-art greenfield built according to best-in-class specifications using the most advanced technology commercially available and staffed with the best and brightest— somehow, its local managers did a terrible job of running Cleveland for a decade and a half.

Magically and mysteriously, the same mill—with the same setup, the same managers, the same everything from the previous year—suddenly rocketed to all-star performer in year 16. A miracle took place. The site manager suddenly became a hero. The engineer touted the quality improvements she made over the past three years. The CEO patted himself on the back for the shrewd capex projects he approved.

Astoundingly, Cleveland's competitiveness stayed up there over the next quarter of a century, despite competing with brand-new facilities using technology and methods never even dreamed of when it was originally constructed. Even after its ROCE begins to fall, the mill's performance after half a century is still better than when it was just five years old. How is this even possible?

Let's look at the math.

What changed in year 15? The original greenfield capex is written off over 15 years. In year 16, the depreciation factor in ROCE's numerator decreased substantially since there is little to nothing left of the original large greenfield capex. Consequently, ROCE's denominator shrunk over the years and was almost gone in year 16.

This happens also if you keep reinvesting in the mill. Despite an almost 40% EBITDA margin in year five when the mill generated its best cash flow, Cleveland's actual performance is obscured by a P&L– and balance sheet–based measure that is unable to reflect what is going on with the business. We used ROCE in this example, but the same story is true when using EVA or any other measure of financial profitability using P&Ls and balance sheets. The effects described above are even more pronounced during times of inflation (where EBITDA inflates; the site's book value and depreciation does not).

Cleveland's ROCE will begin to decline when its EBITDA (part of ROCE's numerator) declines faster than its assets' depreciation and deflation (because the value of the asset base is also diminishing) in its denominator. That is, as the number on top gets smaller faster, the financial ratio begins to get smaller, too, if the numerator cannot keep up with the decline.

Today's profitability measures are driven by a mix of financial facts and accounting rules. Therefore, Quality Pulp Manufacturing cannot use them to consider assets' competitiveness and historic performance. As we've just demonstrated, you could almost say there's an inverse relationship between ROCE and EBITDA margin: the EBITDA margin is great when its ROCE is terrible, and its EBITDA margin declines while its ROCE skyrockets. We've seen some cases where an asset's "true" profitability was solidly 13% while the ROCEs indicated anything from 5 to 60% to, in one extreme case, an astonishing 96%, all due to the reasons explained here.

When we present this to financial experts who've relied on profitability measures as proxies for performance measures, many still hold to the time-honored tradition of believing that the errors somehow self-correct, that the discrepancies between performance and profitability balance out. We're just happy the engineers operating the nuclear plant around our hometown don't run things with the same margin of error.

Why don't we just use the EBITDA margin itself to measure competitiveness and profitability? To a large extent, we can when we're comparing a group of assets that are much the same and have approximately the same technical solutions. The thing is that EBITDA margins exclude capital expenditures. EBITDA margins do not consider how much you had to invest to achieve a certain margin, or how much you are investing. (ROCE tries to do the latter, but fails). We get capital "for free" when looking at an EBITDA margin.

To be thorough, there is, in fact, a way to use profitability measures to accurately measure assets' performance and competitiveness. Here's what it takes:

- The "life" of each asset in the balance sheet (in the asset ledger) must be converted to actual estimated remaining life. This must be continually updated each year with the freshest assumptions on remaining life.
- The balance sheet must contain and have values for all assets in active use.
- The balance sheet must never include any assets not in active use.
- Depreciation for each asset must be recalculated every year based on the newly estimated remaining life which must be updated every year. The desire to have the depreciation of an asset align with previous depreciation levels and for accumulated depreciation to add up to the asset's acquisition amount must be put aside. As such, profitability becomes more of an opinion or subjective conclusion because of the judgment calls used in estimating remaining useful life and the recalculated depreciation—even if such estimates don't match the ones from the year before.

- Straight-line depreciation cannot be used (e.g., an asset worth $100 million being depreciated by $10 million every year for 10 years). Instead, the company must use annuity depreciation. More specifically, the company must use so-called "real annuity" to adjust for inflation every year. The numerator in the ROCE calculation is impacted by inflation, and the denominator must account for that, too.
- The profitability measure used must strictly be the ratio of earnings before interest and taxes (EBIT, with depreciation adjusted as discussed, but no other noncash items) to the fixed assets (with actual estimated remaining life and depreciated as discussed).

If you implement these adjustments, then the ROCE will equal the capital cost if the business is returning an NPV of zero. It will show a ROCE that is twice the capital cost if the business returns twice the value. Now we suddenly have a useful measure directly connected to the logic we have when making value-based decisions. Without all of these adjustments, however, the profitability measure will remain a corrupt proxy of performance. To implement half of these adjustments doesn't make the measure 50% better. Without all of these, the profitability measure is still 100% wrong. (Similar adjustments can be done for EVA—but in reality, this is never done, so they remain corrupt as well.)

## 2. IRR Isn't Related to EBITDA Margins nor ROCE

Between the two of us, we cannot count the number of times we've heard people say, "Oh, if we just invest in projects with a 20% IRR, we'll eventually get a 20% EBITDA margin." That, as well as the statement, "If we invest at 20% IRR, we'll reach 20% ROCE."

As noted previously, just because a drink reads "40% alcohol" doesn't mean the store discounted it 40%. The only thing all these measures have in common is the percentage sign. One doesn't magically result in the other.

The IRR of a capex project is simply the percentage rate of cash flow streams over time that result in an NPV of zero for that capex (based on its delta cash flow). It's a dynamic discounting calculation involving cumulative interest rates. It's tricky to calculate; Microsoft Excel actually performs a number of iterative calculations to arrive at the result. IRR calculations are almost always based on cash flow deltas, which, as we've discussed, don't measure a site's performance. A site's actual cash flow (or EBITDA margin or even ROCE) can be zero, yet the capexes made in that site can have an IRR of 20%, 80%, or even 100%. The numbers aren't incorrect.

A facility's EBITDA margin, on the other hand, is the ratio of earnings (before interest, taxes, depreciation, and amortization) to sales. This is a straightforward calculation; there are no discounting measures and multiyear periods to figure. A facility's EBITDA margin can be zero, where it took all the money the asset's production sales generated to produce the goods in the first place—literally spending every penny the facility makes. At the same time, the capexes in that facility can have an IRR of 200%.

The IRR is based on the difference of the cash flows between doing the capex versus not doing it. How is the IRR supposed to magically translate into an EBITDA margin? Why do people say, "If we invest in projects with a 20% IRR, we'll eventually reach 20% EBITDA margins"? The two measures are completely unrelated; they will never correlate.

A facility's ROCE is more complicated: (EBITDA – depreciation) ÷ the book value of the depreciated assets. Cleveland's ROCE can be zero. At the same time, Cleveland's capexes can have IRRs of 50% in their delta calculations. Again, how are the capexes' IRRs in delta calculations supposed to automatically translate into ROCE? The two measures are completely unrelated.

Believing that IRRs turn into EBITDA margins and ROCEs is exactly that—a belief and a misunderstanding. Unfortunately for the companies and countries of the world, it's a false belief akin to blind faith.

## 3. Capital Investments Aren't for Profitability

Even if Quality Pulp had a way to measure performance, its leadership shouldn't look at capital allocation as a means to improve profitability. Investing to improve profitability can be disastrous, while investing to lower profitability can be fantastic. Companies should focus on maximizing value by way of increasing company cash flow.

Say an entrepreneurially-minded individual invested $10 million to open a Swedish meatball restaurant. Her assumptions came to pass and were realized in the future: her investment returned $30 million in value. As such, the NPV of her investment is $20 million. Success! Her profitability index ($30 million ÷ $10 million) equals 3.0; she tripled her money.

After a few years, she sees a number of customers coming to her restaurant from a neighboring city. She believes that the market exists to support an expansion. Consequently, she opens up another location. At site number two, she invested the same amount of money ($10 million). Her investment returned a value of $20 million, so the NPV is $10 million. Her profitability index there is only 2.0 ($20 million ÷ $10 million).

So, was the second site a good decision?

She certainly thinks so. She invested money and created a lot of value, so she as the shareholder became even richer. However, her company's overall profitability index did fall. Initially, it was 3.0. After her expansion, her total profitability index between the two sites is now just 2.5. Her decision technically lowered the profitability index, despite the fact that it put more cash in her pocket. Even though her company is less profitable than before, she's making more money than ever. In the game of business, this is what really counts.

In fact, she wants to keep opening as many of her Swedish meatball restaurants in the area as possible—right up to the point where the incremental NPV of her last expansion is barely north of zero. As such, she'll get richer and richer as her company becomes less and less profitable—but the profitability is just a consequence of making the right decisions.

Now, let's say a friend of hers sees the entrepreneur's success and is inspired to open the restaurant he's always dreamed of. He invests $10 million in his venture. Unfortunately, he was operating in a saturated market; his business has an NPV of –$5 million. His profitability index is 0.5—he wasted half his money.

Like many restaurateurs, he believes that if he had twice as many locations, he'd sell twice as much, and his money problems would be over. He borrows $10 million from his mother. The NPV from his second location is much better: he only loses $1 million this time and the profitability index is then 0.9. The average profitability of his restaurant group has grown from 0.5 to 0.7!

His second decision increased profitability. Unfortunately, he lost more money.

Her second decision decreased profitability. Fortunately, she made more money.

# 3

# A ~~GOING~~ *GROWING* CONCERN

I n 1994, the Swedish company SCA (then producers of paper, packaging, tissue, and personal care products) faced a paradox. Out of 200 or so production sites, it had invested hundreds of millions of dollars into one mill in particular over several decades. SCA was known for its solid analytical capabilities. Because of this, it was able to identify an issue at this site. The company used the same capex approach it and their peers had used forever. Yet something didn't add up.

Of course, before deciding to implement any one capex, the company's leaders calculated the project's IRR. Over the previous 15 years, they estimated their capex projects would, on average, achieve a 40% IRR. Time proved them correct. Their other predictions about each capex project generally came to be. For instance, if they estimated a 3% reduction in energy consumption or streamlined 10 positions, their capex projects delivered on those expectations. Operation's ability to implement improvements was solid. Furthermore, to evaluate each capex's success, they calculated the site's ROCE. Over those same 15 years under review, the site delivered a ROCE of 25%, exceeding company targets by a comfortable margin. Anyone in the pulp and paper industry would agree the IRRs and ROCEs were impressive numbers. Everything about the site's capexes delivered as promised. It was a well-functioning site by all means—yet by 1994, SCA could see that the mill averaged zero in accumulated cash flows over those past 15 years. Analysis after analysis yielded the same results. The average cash flow for the past decade-and-a-half was practically nothing. The mill didn't add one dime to the company's bank account despite all the successful work.

One of SCA's foremost business controllers, Erik Ottosson, happened to come across a recently completed graduate thesis on capex calculations written by one Fredrik Weissenrieder at the Gothenburg School of Economics in western Sweden. In the thesis, the graduate student questioned why companies used a measure like IRR to estimate future capex performance but then used a fundamentally different concept like ROCE to evaluate past performance. The economic theories behind the two are completely unrelated. (See our dedicated primer to this issue in Chapter 2.) Why evaluate the past with one theory but use another for the future?

The day before the student's graduation, SCA brought him in to give them a different perspective on their paradox. He spent four months digging through records and cash flows stretching decades back, creating countless spreadsheets. In addition to his quantitative research, he also performed qualitative research. (In other words, he got out from behind his computer screen to walk around and talk to people.) That's where he found what was later to be the most revelatory piece of insight he would come across in the whole project.

In a conversation with the local mill's controller, he asked, "What is your line of reasoning when investing in the mill?"

The controller replied, "We invest according to the going concern principle."

Coming from a background in corporate finance and economics, not accounting, Weissenrieder had never heard the term. In an unprecedented move for the consulting profession, he confessed his ignorance and asked the controller to explain what that meant.

"Oh, it means we invest based on the assumption that operations will continue indefinitely. We invest to keep the mill running," the controller answered.

At the time, it made sense to the new graduate. It would take him another four years to discover that the going concern principle was one of the key reasons why so many companies make suboptimal capital allocation decisions. They act as if their facilities will operate forever instead of planning for their inevitable obsolescence.

> *The going concern principle fails to take macro-level economics into account.*

## INEVITABLE INNOVATION

You can't improve a given system if you can't agree on the goal of the system. We have regularly observed a disconnect between the strategic goal of companies' production systems (maximizing shareholder value) and the tactical decisions within those production systems (piecemeal capital investments to maintain operations). A production portfolio can aim for one or the other but not both.

> *You cannot maximize shareholder value with a going concern approach.*

The going concern principle isn't a long-term strategy. It doesn't account for the macro-level economic forces of the free market. In simpler terms: the status quo can't compete against innovation. For example, in 1916, it took 1,000 people to bring the same amount of timber out from Swedish forests as it did just one person 100 years later. The companies that assumed they would be a going concern forever and invested accordingly in their forestry operations went out of business. Those that stayed in business kept adopting new technologies and new methods, leaving old equipment behind and investing in new machinery, producing more and more with less and less. You can keep things as they are, or you can keep up with the competition. You can't do both.

Another reason why the going concern principle isn't a viable long-term strategy is that companies cannot afford to invest to keep all their sites competitive. There is a reason for why they can't: they are not supposed to. That is not supposed to make financial sense in a market economy in an industry with technology changes. Choices have to be made.

In Figure 2.1, we presented the competitiveness of a single site over time. At the end of its life cycle, a site reaches obsolescence. At the ground level, this means technology and processes in an existing system will gradually become less and less competitive as the latest technology and work methods continually improve and are being implemented by the competition. But the going concern principle ignores this reality. It assumes that an asset, be it a production line or an entire site, will continue to operate as is forever.

At the aggregate level, this is what happens. In the 1970s, Sweden had 240 large sawmills. Forty years later, it had half that. (A large number closed while a handful of greenfields and brownfields opened, resulting in a net loss of half.) Yet those 120 sawmills generate *twice* as much lumber than the original 240. The existing sawmills are on average four times larger, capacitywise. The process of innovation—better technology, better methods, better processes, better training, and so forth—always results in the ability to do more with less.

Industry professionals understand this. In any given industry, consolidation happens over time.* However, there seems to be a

---

* It should be noted that there is nothing inherent in our logic that says that the change always goes in the direction of fewer and larger production units (even though most of the industries that we have worked for have gone that way). The change could just as well go the other way—more production units that are smaller, cheaper, and more agile. Either way, the going concern principle is still a flawed approach.

disconnect between the abstract idea of these free-market forces and the day-to-day reality of capex decision-making. While executives understand that macro-level economics eventually results in consolidation at the theoretical level, it is quite rare that they plan for this inevitability at the decision-making level. Put this way: For those 120 sawmills that closed, how many were run according to the going concern principle even five years before their closure? How many were operated as if they would continue forever? Most likely, all of them because companies don't have long-term production system plans.

## THE CREATIVE DESTRUCTION FUNNEL

In Macroeconomics 101, we learn that over time the costs of labor and land have historically trended upward (also accounting for inflation). In some markets, wages may stagnate for a time, even decades, but overall, full labor costs including benefits rise.* Historically, if a country prospers but the labor force does not get its share of the growth in prosperity, there will be backlash at some point.

Because of free-market competition and productivity gains, the real price of manufactured goods tends to go down (again, accounting for inflation). For example, there was a time when a TV was a substantial household purchase. If the screen cracked, people would take it to a TV repair shop. When this happens today, we don't even bother trying to fix the screen. We know that we can get a bigger screen with higher resolution for the same price we paid for the broken TV, if not cheaper. The only time these economic conditions don't hold true is when there are artificial mechanisms

---

* This assumption has been under debate and challenged in particular in the United States where nonqualified labor earnings seem to have stalled in real terms for a number of decades. Accounting for full employment costs, including benefits, changes the picture, however. It can also be shown that during this period the cost of labor has increased faster than inflation. In addition, the expectations for future wage cost raises have increased significantly.

in place, such as the economic control in the former Soviet Union or North Korea, legal monopolies, or when companies engage in illegal price fixing through cartels.

There was one time we came across a long-term fixed-price contract situation with one paper machine in particular. Our client's customer had entered into a multidecade contract for paper that compensated for inflation. This guaranteed a stable EBITDA margin for that one paper mill. This worked out well for the paper manufacturer since its asset wasn't subject to free market forces. For its customer's shareholders, however, this arrangement destroyed a substantial amount of value. The same product was available cheaper from other suppliers and would only get cheaper in real terms. Meanwhile, the customer was stuck paying the same rate for more than 20 years.

On the whole, leadership understands and accepts these trends at the macroeconomic level. Few, however, think about how this applies at the company level and in decision-making. For some reason, many professionals believe their in-place decision-making structures are set up to address this, but they are not. People trust the processes, which they should be able to do. These processes have always been there, and their peers use more or less the same processes. However, when a company creates a financial plan and its projections, it is unusual to see the company assume that the cost of raw materials will increase while the relative price of their production products will decrease.

The graph in Figure 3.1 depicts those two economic forces at work in the case of the 240 Swedish sawmills consolidating into just 120 sites.

The sawmill industry became four times as efficient over four decades from a production-per-site point of view. Did the industry improve profitability on the whole? Of course not. In a market economy, an industry does not keep the benefits from technology developments and other productivity improvements; it is given away to the customers. This is why democracies allow for and thrive under capitalism and free markets, if a functional legal framework for it is in place. This is economic growth. Relative to input costs going up, output prices go down: the two free-market forces are shown as literally squeezing the number of production assets in the industry. This forms what we call the "creative destruction funnel." "Creative destruction" is a term coined by economist Joseph Schumpeter and refers to the ceaseless product and process innovations by which new production facilities replace outdated units. In Schumpeter's own words, creative destruction is "the essential fact about capitalism."* Capitalism is never stationary and always evolving.

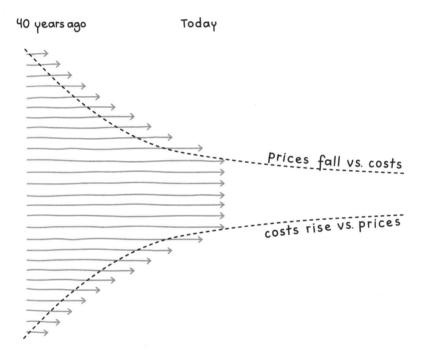

The least competitive sawmills (those near the edges of the funnel) are killed off in the business equivalent of survival of the fittest. This is simply the nature of the free market. Like any force of nature, it cannot be stopped. The most competitive sawmills

---

* Schumpeter, J. *Capitalism, Socialism, and Democracy.* New York: Harper & Brothers, 1942.

(those at the center) are far more efficient, using fewer resources to make more and higher-quality wood products more efficiently. These sawmills are the ones likely to survive a few cycles, while others are not. The great artist Pablo Picasso pointed out, "Every act of creation is first an act of destruction." The creative destruction funnel works like a literal funnel, with more and more product flowing more quickly through fewer and fewer production sites—the market economy at work.

### Is It a Bad Thing to Lose 120 Sawmills?

Economically and environmentally, losing 120 sawmills is great. Sweden's sawmill industry needs fewer inputs such as labor and capital to produce more and higher-quality wood products. This means a smaller industry footprint. The resources spared can be put to better use elsewhere.

At the company level, this is fantastic. It creates consolidation opportunities and more capital allocation options, allowing the company to meet market demand at a fraction of the costs.

From the country's point of view, this is fantastic. Sweden makes more with fewer resources, and that is called growth. Resources are released, money is made anyway, and the consolidation creates a foundation for growth elsewhere in society. Those nations that recognize this is a healthy process for them will be healthier than others. Societies that ensure that people are placed at other in-demand jobs and locations will fare even better and face less resistance to the creative destruction process. Capitalism at its best.

Returning to our example of Quality Pulp Manufacturing, Cleveland sits near the edge of the industry's creative destruction funnel, as do all C sites. Albuquerque and its fellow star performers would sit in the very center. Between the center and the edges sit Baton Rouge and other such middling production sites.

Through our experience, we have observed that companies spend a disproportionate amount of the capex budget on their B and C sites (not recognizing them for what they are) three to eight years before they're forced to close them. In Figure 3.2, this is represented by the shaded areas—the period of time just before leadership realizes a production site cannot be saved.

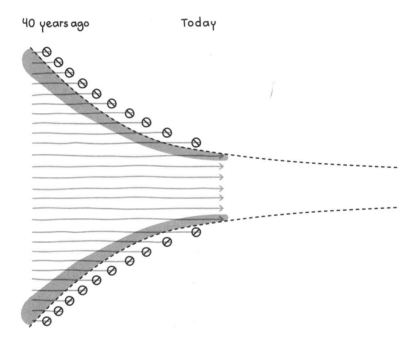

Referring back to Table 2.1 on the three different site categories:

| Site Category | A | B | C |
|---|---|---|---|
| Annual Capex Invested | 20% | 75% | 5% |
| Management Attention | 5% | 65% | 30% |

As discussed previously, capex as it's practiced today results in directing most of a company's resources in capital and management's attention to the sites closest to obsolescence. Why? Well, according to conventional capex calculations and communication around capex decisions, all the lights are green:

1. The capex required is quite obvious and there is little debate about what is needed. The issue the capex solves has typically been on the table for one to five years. The technical solution isn't rocket science, as it has been used everywhere else for years.
2. Because the equipment being replaced is so old, the cash flow deltas are large and the paybacks are short. The NPVs and IRRs are unbeatable.
3. The ROCE for the site may be something like 15 to 20% (by this point, almost all the assets still in use have been written off), which is above the company average. This is not because the site is actually competitive within the industry. In truth, the site's competitiveness is terrible.

A capex project where all lights are green—an obvious issue, proven solution, fast payback, and a high ROCE—are actually red flags to us.

In 2008, a company announced the closure of a mill in Sweden, after analyzing the company's entire portfolio of production sites. In its last year, the mill's ROCE was 18%—an impressive yet ultimately irrelevant number. A site's individual performance doesn't matter in isolation, only in the grand scheme of an entire production system.

A bad process is worse than no process at all. To paraphrase that for our purposes: a bad capex budgeting process (the capex selection process) is worse than no process at all. With a completely random system, the law of averages means a company will have a good mix of hits and misses. With a bad system, you systemize the errors, and then the system itself amplifies the errors. Quality Pulp's capex budgeting process has more or less institutionalized value destruction with its needs-driven, bottom-up approach to capex budgeting. In the real world, today's capex processes skew the true picture, obscuring the best opportunities and distorting the worst. This is how economic value is destroyed, not only at the company level, but at an industry level as well as that of the national economy.

> *Companies survive* despite *their current capex processes—not because of them.*

# CAPEX NEEDS VERSUS CAPITAL ALLOCATION OPPORTUNITIES

Economics is the study of resource allocation. Economic value comes from allocation decisions. Nobel Prize–winning economist Paul Samuelson wrote, "Economics is a choice between alternatives all the time. Those are the trade-offs."* Value is either created or destroyed by those decisions. It isn't until later that it becomes apparent whether they are the right decisions or not. Regardless, it's at the decision point that value is essentially created or destroyed. What happens afterward is merely the consequence of that decision.

In manufacturing companies, resource allocation *is* capital allocation. Virtually everything that happens, from doing your best to improve sales and marketing to human resources and IT, is a consequence of a handful of strategic decisions. If the leaders make the

---

* Samuelson, P. "The Basics of Economics with Paul Samuelson." Interview by Paul Solman. *PBS News Hour.* 2009.

right strategic decisions, the company will create economic value for the shareholders. If they don't, they will destroy shareholder value by way of wasting company capital. It is often said that you can't undo a bad decision. The good thing is that you can't undo a good decision either (but it can be mismanaged).

It may be difficult to believe, but some people in capital-intensive companies do not understand that it is capital allocation decisions that create or destroy value. We come across professionals like this sometimes. They see capexes purely as a "cost of doing business," like a penalty. Something they are forced to do, but actually don't want to. They shrink the capex budget as much as they can, and sometimes even claim to be "world-class regarding capexes" because they spend less than any of their peers. These companies will eventually fade out or implode. They will certainly never appear successful for more than a few quarters or maybe a handful of years.

It is not a given that a company will create economic value for the shareholders, not at all. That is one of the large misunderstandings within corporations. Half of all decisions create value, but the other half do not by definition, because the average is your opportunity cost (the industry's stock market index, represented in the cost of equity portion in your weighted average cost of capital [WACC], is your opportunity cost). This means, if you are a company that has followed an index for 10 years or so, then you succeeded in half of your capital expenditure and you did not succeed with the other half. Half will have a positive NPV while the other half will end up with a negative NPV; the total NPV equals zero.

Upgrading to new enterprise resource management software might help a company become more efficient. Funding a substantial culture initiative might help employees become more effective. Automating quality control might improve operations. These actions are important, to be sure; they're necessary in order to survive. But these activities do not create economic value in manufacturing companies; they save or rescue economic value (made from previous decisions) that otherwise would have been destroyed.

All companies must manage large strategic decisions made in the past (such as a new site) in the best possible way. They will always work on improving things (or rather, stopping things from eroding), but starting from where? From the starting level when the strategic decision of building the site was made. Again, value is created or destroyed when the larger strategic decision is made. Everything after that is just making the best of it all. We don't mean to diminish the effort it takes to do that. We're merely pointing out that value comes from a strategic decision, not from the millions of tasks that come after it. Those subsequent efforts very rarely—you could even say never—create new value. When they made the strategic decision, the original decision makers assumed that their predecessors would put forth their best efforts. They had already factored that into their decision-making process. They assumed that the managers who come after them will continually improve the site, so those improvements do not add value—they maintain the original value.

No matter how efficient a manufacturing company is, the tactical-level decisions made after the larger strategic decision cannot compensate for the macroeconomic forces at play. A manufacturing company (or any company, for that matter) can't "cost save" its way to success. If a CEO says, "We'll cut fixed costs by 5%," it might be good news, but it does not change the direction or value of the company. The company is just doing what all its peers are doing, what is expected from them. In fact, if companies have 5% of "fat" they can take out, they may be behind their peers. Why do they have that much to cut in the first place? Shareholders expect their company's management to hold costs at an optimal level. What else would the company be doing, if not aiming for the best and most sustainable margins? An announcement like this is as newsworthy as the CEO declaring that the company is striving to make a higher profit. Every one of their competitors is trying to lower fixed costs. None of those efforts create shareholder value, but they may reveal a historic pattern of destroying it.

A manufacturing company can't sell more to reach success either because that is expected from all the players in an industry. It must create economic value at least as well as its competitors to survive. Its ability to create economic value was set many years before, when leadership chose to allocate capital in a certain way. Leadership picked a game out of the playbook, and the company's managers today are faced with playing it the best way they know how. In virtually every organization, leadership's most important job is often creating resilience for hard-to-predict, long-term macroeconomic changes. Leadership must spend its time designing the future company via a highly organized, holistic process. That is not being done in companies today because they are relying on an incorrectly designed, purely tactical capex allocation process to do so.

Companies that succeed in the long term are managed by leaders whose capital allocation decisions consistently generate net value creation on the whole. (All companies make both value-creating and value-destroying decisions. It's a question of which ones outweigh the others.) Companies that fail are those that spend most of their capex budget ineffectively.

With an industry average, by definition half of the industry's capacity is above average; half is below. Similar to the stock market, though, this doesn't mean that half of companies are above average. When a mutual fund manager picks stocks, she doesn't expect half of the companies she picks to deliver half of the fund's performance. From experience, she knows that some stocks will perform poorly. Most will perform right at or slightly below average. She's counting on a handful of stellar performers to compensate for all the other stocks' dismal performance.

At a macro level, most companies lag behind the industry's average competitiveness. It's the few successful outliers that raise the average because of their disproportionate success. In absolute terms, a company can succeed a lot more than it is ever possible to lose. There is a floor to losing, called bankruptcy; there is not a ceiling to success. This is true whether we're talking about an industry, venture capital investments, or the stock market. A handful of companies are far above average; most are below. The scale factor is easily 10:1, where one company or investment is worth as much as the next 10 combined.

All of this begs the question: How can leadership better identify value-creating opportunities and avoid those that destroy economic value? Perhaps a more nuanced perspective should be considered. It's not only a matter of whether a decision resulted in value creation or not; there's the issue of whether it was the best decision out of all decisions possible. "Good" might have been good enough 40 years ago, but in today's global, competitive, transparent, and digitized world, companies' capital allocation must go from "good" to "great." It's a matter of survival.

A company can remain a good—or even lousy—entity if it has a monopoly or lives in a closed or semiclosed economy with high import barriers. A closed or semi-closed economy negatively impacts the nation, its citizens, the environment, and often even a company's shareholders—but a company can continue to function as long as it is propped up. This means that even "surviving" isn't enough to declare a company a good one.

If Quality Pulp Manufacturing approves a series of capexes that result in higher company accumulated discounted cash flows, then it creates economic value. But was there a better strategy that would have generated even more? That is, the company may have created shareholder value, but did it create as much value as it possibly could have?

Economics is the science of trade-offs. The decision to spend a dollar on one thing is simultaneously the decision to *not* spend that dollar on an infinite number of other things. These other potential opportunities are forgone. Economists call these "opportunity costs." Practically speaking, these opportunity costs are quantified in the company's capital allocation process as the WACC. We can subjectively discuss opportunity costs, of course, but we need to quantify the opportunity costs in a practical way for capex calculations.

---

### Capex Strategy Keystone

*Use the WACC—not inflated hurdle rates. The cost of capital isn't something a company chooses; it's based on data from capital markets.*

---

If the leadership at Quality Pulp decides to approve a $100 million capex project because it has a positive NPV, it is in effect deciding not to use that $100 million on a hundred other potential capex projects (not to mention the opportunity to pay it out in dividends or to repay financing debt). The question is whether that $100 million decision was the best call.

With the way capex is practiced today, that's often not leadership's perspective. From a holistic viewpoint, the questions are seldom: Is this the best and highest use of company capital? Will this provide us with the best possible future company cash flow? That would require a systems view of their production portfolio. Instead, when it comes to capex it's a binary, black-or-white tactical question: Is this a good capex project? The better question would be: Out of all the capex strategies or project combinations we could possibly pursue over time, which one would result in the greatest amount of long-term company cash flow? Which capex projects to prioritize and how to execute them is simply a consequence of answering that question, an output of the capex strategy.

Of course, to answer that question, leadership would need a tool capable of modeling its entire production system and then simulate multiple potential capex strategies and the resulting accumulated cash flows from each one. Then, and only then, could leadership compare competing capex strategies against each other.

> *Companies don't have a capex strategy.*
> *They have a needs- and opportunity-driven capital budgeting process that focuses on tactical choices.*

For example, Quality Pulp could invest $100 million in a capex to expand capacity in Baton Rouge, but is that the best possible use of shareholder capital? What if the company instead debottlenecked a production line in Albuquerque, invested in a new capability in one of their other B sites, consolidated Cleveland's capacity by adding two additional lines in another A site, and optimized all production lines? Would that be a better use of $100 million? Typically, management does not know. The board that approves the large capex doesn't know. In fact, educating the board needs to be a top priority for any CEO serious on implementing a systems approach to capex allocation, as Annica Bresky, president and CEO of Stora Enso, discusses in the Afterword of this book. The question does not get asked often enough, nor is it analyzed in sufficient depth: Are these capex investments the best use of shareholder capital?

# CAPEX VERSUS CAPITAL ALLOCATION

In a given corporation, the board of directors sets a somewhat arbitrary amount of capital dedicated to capital expenditures. Companies need to replace equipment, comply with safety and environment standards, and more. Above that minimum level, it is implicitly assumed that the company's leadership can create more shareholder value via capital investments in the existing business than it can by:

1. Paying dividends
2. Buying back shares
3. Organically expanding
4. Acquiring another company
5. Entering new businesses

The first two alternatives are fairly straightforward. If the company cannot create higher returns via capexes than its WACC, then it should issue additional dividends and/or buy back company shares. We are not talking about finding delta calculations in the capex budget that beat the WACC; those can always be found and especially those that destroy value. We mean capex *strategies* that beat the WACC.

The amount dedicated for capex is sometimes related to the company's depreciation. We believe this is a certain path to underinvesting and ultimately ruining the company. Depreciation levels cannot predict company opportunities, and it is a number that doesn't at all reflect inflation in equipment over time.

The third option—organically expanding—can be quite speculative unless you grow with the market's growth. For a company to grow faster than the market is growing (and make money doing so) is not easy. The likely case is that the company has a competitive edge only within its current field of operations, even if most companies don't. And there is just a small chance for success unless the company has a strong competitive advantage. Beyond this, in manufacturing companies in particular, shareholders usually aren't comfortable with company leadership launching into businesses, products, or markets where the company doesn't already have a clear competitive advantage of some kind, be it through technology, knowledge, intellectual property, or something else. Neither do shareholders usually smile on commodity companies vertically integrating by buying downstream operations and thereby launching into completely unfamiliar types of operational cultures.*

## Why Upstream Companies Should Stay in Their Lanes

Vertically integrating by buying or expanding into downstream operations leads a company into markets of higher added value products. This term "higher added value" is often confusing because it is misleading. As we've discussed so far, shareholder value is added through higher cash flows. Simply operating in a market of products with "higher added value" doesn't mean that more value is added to the company.

The "usefulness" or "utility" of the product for the customer is higher, sure, and that is what the term points to. The end customer wants to buy furniture from IKEA, not the raw wood it is built from, but that's different from adding value to the shareholder, and that additional usefulness costs money. From our observations and firsthand knowledge of commodity companies going head-to-head with specialist consumer companies, all too often the result is negative value creation.

Commodity companies often struggle with vertical integration. Downstream, closer to the end user, the market moves faster. This requires a shift in organizational culture, one of being more responsive to market changes, to be

---

* As always, there are exceptions to the rule. We have clients that have succeeded tremendously in terms of value creation with integrated downstream operations.

much closer to the customer on an even perhaps daily basis, to be agile, to be prepared to pivot. Commodity industries operate on a more long-term basis, where markets and technology change more slowly. As such, commodity companies' cultures often clash with downstream operations.

In many commodity industries, companies face further challenges when trying to compete downstream because those competitors are often family-owned companies. These types of companies rarely demand the same rates of return as a publicly traded company or private equity firm does. Because of this, we have seen plenty of corporate managers whose perspective is that these family companies are ruining the market by adding capacity as well as operating where they simply can't compete.

Put succinctly: moving into higher value-added products often leads to lower added value for shareholders.*

In general, it's a good business practice to maximize the potential in your current market before speculating with shareholder capital in other businesses. It is not as exciting for the leadership and doesn't make for a splashy headline, but managing a company should focus on maximizing shareholder value, not playing games with other people's money.

Too many times we have seen where companies have acquired another company instead of fixing their current system of facilities. After the acquisition—which statistically in most cases is a poor one—they have no money left to fix the facilities they previously had, much less the newly acquired ones.

---

* See previous footnote on exceptions.

## A Short Note on Growth in Manufacturing

We sometimes hear of CEOs making companywide declarations such as, "We're going to grow by 5% in all markets every year for the next five years!"

A CEO may believe this is possible. The concern is whether this is beneficial, and whether the existing asset base (in combination with the strategic options this growth can create for the asset base) is fit for growth *and* creates value. Many managers have the opinion that growth is always a good thing, that growth equals value creation. If the goal of the company is to maximize market share, then perhaps growth is a good thing. But in most countries, the CEO has a fiduciary responsibility to maximize shareholder value, which may or may not be correlated to market share. The goal of the company should not be to grow as big as possible, but to create as much cash flow in the long term as possible.*

These CEOs should say instead, "We're going to maximize long-term shareholder value by growing where we can create value!" It doesn't sound as impressive, but it is more correct. That's the mission; if growth occurs, it's simply a means to an end—not an end unto itself. The CEO could also say something along these lines: "The market is growing 3% every year. We have created an overall strategy that will allow us to gain market share while also increasing shareholder value creation."

By definition, half of all expansions deliver above-average expectations (positive NPV). That means that the other half miss expectations (negative NPV). Some industries have low barriers to entry and are too easy to expand into or convert assets into. There, one could claim that the majority of expansion projects have negative NPV (and penalize all

---

* Admittedly this could look different in the very early stages of establishing a market in the life of a startup.

others already in that market on their way to join them). The ones that succeed combine the right mix of competitive edge, healthy company cash flow, good access to raw material, the right people (able to develop and execute on attractive capex opportunities), and ideal location. If these factors are present and if the goal is to maximize shareholder value, then a profitable expansion may be possible.

How should a company measure value creation from its capex projects?

In previous chapters, we discussed two fundamental flaws in capex today:

- Performance is calculated with cash flow deltas— despite the fact that a capital expenditure in a site with a negative cash flow will still have a positive delta. In fact, its delta (perceived benefit) will be larger than in better performing sites.
- Each capex project is analyzed in isolation as if it were totally independent of other capital assets, production systems, business situations, and capex decisions in the short and long term.

The purpose of a corporation isn't to maximize the performance of each individual capital project or asset. It's to maximize the performance of the company as a whole. Those are not the same thing. They are two different methods, mathematically. They will deliver two different results, even if the input data is the same.

*Maximizing the performance of each capital project or asset ≠ maximizing the performance of the company.*

The "company" is a production system that can be composed of dozens, hundreds, or even thousands of interdependent individual production assets. A systems view prioritizes the needs and opportunities of the system (aka the company) over the needs and opportunities of the system's components (aka individual sites, production lines, etc.). The "needs" of individual assets are necessary from a going concern perspective: Cleveland needs a major capex to keep running.

But does the company need Cleveland?

The company doesn't exist to serve Cleveland; Cleveland exists to serve the company. Quality Pulp shouldn't do what's best for Cleveland, Baton Rouge, nor Albuquerque. Quality Pulp should do what's best for the company. What happens afterward are the consequences of that perspective. The capital expenditures spent in its 10 mills should be determined by the system's needs. As it stands today, however, the tail is wagging the dog.

## Beyond Maximizing Shareholder Value

Increasingly, people mention to us that maximizing shareholder value is an antiquated approach to business. To this, we say two things:

- First: when it comes to capital allocation, shareholders must be the focus since they—and no one else—legally own the capital being allocated.
- Second: our method can include multidimensional measures of success.

For example, if a corporation has a goal of becoming carbon neutral, it needs a tool to evaluate how best to reach that goal. One solution might be to reduce waste in its supply chain, thereby reducing its footprint by 5%. But what if the better way to achieve that goal is to improve production margins, providing enough cash flow to buy offset credits that reduces the company footprint by 10%? Or perhaps a public utility company needs to figure out the most resource-efficient way to fulfill expectations to supply water or electricity. The utility company is a complex system with many opportunities and whole system alternatives with various assumptions, depending on which one is chosen. The only way to evaluate these competing alternative strategies is with a method that can take all such factors into consideration.

The performance of capex projects—indeed, the performance of a company's portfolio of production assets—must be measured with metrics that reflect actual company performance. That cannot be cash flow deltas, as they are relative measures that use themselves as a reference. Operational cash flows, on the other hand, do not. Cold, hard company cash is an absolute measure. As simple as it may seem, our process is premised on a straightforward question: How can a company's capital assets generate the most money for the company? Note that the question is not: What are the best deltas from individually calculated capexes? That perspective can never maximize company value and cash flow. The math simply doesn't work out.

Make no mistake about it, capex investments are the strongest out of the few true competitive advantages left in capital-intensive industries. Packaging, petrochemicals, oil and gas production, energy production, wood production, pulp and paper, mining, steel, food processing—our clients work in sectors so commoditized, so competitive, and so global that each of them faces virtually identical challenges as their peers. They have access to the same brilliant talent pools, the same capital markets, and the same vendors offering the same advances in technology. Because of the extremely high barriers to entry—needing a billion dollars to build a greenfield site, for example—the number of players in any one market doesn't change often or quickly. The only real difference between those that thrive and those that simply survive comes down to just one question: How do they allocate their resources? Most specifically, how do they allocate management's attention and shareholder capital? Doubt, regret, and confusion have no place at this level of survival, and yet these are exactly the thoughts and feelings we've seen from scores of our clients making capex decisions for hundreds of production sites across six continents. Everything looks right, but something's still off.

Many try to improve their capex decision-making process, yet feel they've made minor adjustments instead of major strides. (You cannot improve the conventional approach to the capital allocation process.) They all want to feel more confident they made the right call, but instead often experience the same uncertainty as the executives from Chapter 3 who in 1994 faced paradoxical contradictions with one of their mills—a "high" ROCE on great projects but no cash flow. SCA had the expertise to realize there was a problem and it searched for a radical solution. Unfortunately, many of its peers don't even realize they have a problem, so they keep pouring millions of dollars into walking corpses.

## Why Companies Exist

Legally, companies exist to manage and allocate the owners' capital. The objective of implementing a holistic capex strategy process is to institutionalize the ability to maximize company cash flow long term and without interruption through much smarter capital allocation means. A company's ability to generate cash flow and value is determined when major decisions are made. For industrial companies, this happens when major capital-related decisions are being made, such as expansions, mergers and acquisitions (M&A), consolidations, and so on. The number of major strategic capital-related decisions are a very small proportion of all the decisions being made (0.1–5%, typically), but the absolute value tends to be large. This is where value (NPV) is created or lost!

All other decisions (95–99.9%, typically) are a consequence of past and current major capital-related decisions. They do not create value; they are made to rescue or fulfill the value already promised when approving the major capital-related decisions. As discussed earlier, all other activities—creating business plans, developing market strategies, implementing productivity improvement projects, refinancing, recruiting the right people, working like crazy, and more—are also there to deliver the value originally promised when the company made a major capital-related decision.

## EVERY COMPANY IS CAPITAL INTENSIVE

While our clients are generally classified as capital intensive, we argue that every company should have an explicit capital allocation strategy regardless of its industry. We've found that the less capital intensive managers believe their companies to be, the greater the capital allocation opportunities there are.

Let's go back to our example of Swedish sawmills. Compared to other industrial sites, sawmills are comparatively small. In some pulp and paper companies, they're even treated as part of the wood fiber supply chain and considered a cost center. As such, the parent companies have never viewed their sawmills through a strategic lens as something that can or should be improved. That is, sawmills aren't viewed the way they deserve to be—as a business. Any strategic opportunities that exist have been consistently overlooked or dismissed. Because of this, we've found many capex strategy opportunities that resulted in either high cash flows for the sawmills or greater cost savings for their parent companies. More than once, our method has led to increasing operational cash flows in these types of lower capital intensity companies or divisions by 100%, whereas with traditional capital-intensive operations such as steel or pulp mills, we see something more like 30–60% cash flow increases.

A company is generally considered capital intensive when a large proportion of its sales is spent on maintaining equipment, machinery, and capital assets. For instance, a company that spends 10% of its annual sales revenue on capexes over a life cycle. To compensate for this, its EBITDA margins have to be higher than a typical company's. A typical breakdown might look like this:

| Sales | $1,000 |
|---|---|
| Costs | –$600 |
| EBITDA | $400 |
| EBITDA margin | 40% |
| Capex | –$100 |
| Cash flow | $300 |
| Capex % of sales | 10% |

With an EBITDA margin of 40%, if the company sold $1,000 worth of services, then its costs would be $600—a $400 EBITDA margin. However, 10% of its sales revenue (or $100) must be reinvested in capexes to maintain operations long term. That $400 EBITDA quickly becomes $300 of operational cash flow. If this company's EBITDA margin were 8%, it would quickly fold. There wouldn't be enough EBITDA to pay for the necessary capexes and still generate additional cash flow.

Let's compare this to a company in another less capital-intensive industry that usually spends only 2.5% of its sales revenue on capital expenditures to maintain operations long term. We should expect its resulting EBITDA margin to be lower. (Otherwise, with fatter margins, other companies would quickly move in. The resulting competition would quickly drive profits down to an equilibrium price.)

| Sales | $1,000 |
|---|---|
| Costs | −$900 |
| EBITDA | $100 |
| EBITDA margin | 10% |
| Capex | −$25 |
| Cash flow | $75 |
| Capex % of sales | 2.5% |

This company, too, sold $1,000 worth of goods and services, but it had to spend $900 in costs to do so. That leaves an EBITDA of $100. However, its managers only need to spend $25 (2.5% of sales) on capexes, leaving $75 in operational cash flow.

It's easy to see why a higher EBITDA margin usually goes hand in hand with a higher capex-to-sales ratio. But instead of looking at capex as a percentage of sales, let's look at capex as a percentage of EBITDA and cash flow.

| Sales | $1,000 |
|---|---|
| Costs | −$600 |
| EBITDA | $400 |
| EBITDA margin | 40% |
| Capex | −$100 |
| Cash flow | $300 |
| Capex % of sales | 10% |
| Capex % of EBITDA | 25% |
| Capex % of cash flow | 33% |

| Sales | $1,000 |
|---|---|
| Costs | −$900 |
| EBITDA | $100 |
| EBITDA margin | 10% |
| Capex | −$25 |
| Cash flow | $75 |
| Capex % of sales | 2.5% |
| Capex % of EBITDA | 25% |
| Capex % of cash flow | 33% |

Although the capital-intensive company spends more of its sales revenue on capex, it spends the same percentage of its EBITDA *and* the same percentage of its operating cash flow on capex. From the standpoint of value creation and the capex impact on value creation, these two companies are identical. That's why we believe what differentiates capital-intensive companies from others is the amount of capexes compared against its EBITDA and cash flows—not as a percentage of sales. And this percentage should be similar over a life cycle since excess profitability/loss will otherwise be a fact. In the long run, in a free market economy, no industries shall inherently be more or less profitable than others.

> *Capital intensity is measured by capex versus EBITDA— not capex versus sales.*

We are often brought in to deal with mills in the pulp, paper, packaging, and steel industries. Our engagements typically don't look at downstream operations (e.g., converting plants or building materials) since that's considered less capital intensive. Companies often do not see the importance of allocating capital efficiently in those businesses. Our experience shows an enormous amount of value lost from poor capital allocation there—a greater percentage than in the "capital-intensive" operations. Of course, that also means greater opportunities, too. Again, this stems from how those companies or divisions are perceived. Or, rather, overlooked.

> *Capital allocation decisions are what design companies and create shareholder value.*

In those companies' defense, downstream operations are generally more cost intensive, customer driven, and more—but again, that doesn't mean less capital intensive. Capital allocation strategies and decisions look different between larger upstream facilities and downstream operations. In a steel or paper mill, for example, typical issues are increasing or decreasing capacity, deciding on closures, more "big-ticket" items like massive boilers, questions of long-term competitiveness, and adequate access to raw materials. Contrast that to a converting plant or food-processing factory; those issues are typically more mundane, such as site location, freight costs, customer service and responsiveness, roof maintenance and repairs, workforce shifts, improving competencies, and keeping and hiring the right people. All of these decisions, in the larger sites and the smaller downstream plants, revolve around asset and capex decisions. A 10% loss because of poor capital allocation is still 10%, regardless of how many zeroes that represents.

> *Capital should be treated with the same care in every company and division—regardless of perceived capital intensiveness*

This first part of our book has focused on today's capex process—both how it is viewed and how it is practiced.

Virtually every company approaches the capital expenditure process the same way. Local sites submit capex requests, the numbers are crunched, and the projects with the highest returns and shortest paybacks get funded. That's on top of the "must-do" capexes for environmental and safety requirements that simply can't be ignored. If the company works with detailed capex budgets, the funded project list is drawn up and then the budget is approved and labeled "Capex Budget 20xx." Other organizations simply rely on increasing or decreasing last year's spend to be the "allowance" for this year. Still other companies use even more simplistic methods such as allowing for a certain portion of depreciation to be invested.

Companies rarely call this their capex strategy, which is just as well. What they have is not a strategy, but a series of tactical decisions over a limited time period. A strategy should intentionally design the future of the company; a company should not unintentionally and unknowingly be designed by a collection of bottom-up production needs and opportunities. A capex strategy will lay out decisions over many years, not just for one to three years as a budget does. High-level strategic decisions should dictate which capital expenditures are needed and where.

After those four months in 1994 at SCA described earlier, Fredrik presented the findings of his study of the mill to the mill's management. Right after the last slide there was a short silence.

Then somebody said, "I have never seen a mill's financial outcome being presented in this way before. On top of that, you say that we have not been making decisions in an optimal way. The thing is, I believe you after having seen the presentation. My question to you is: How should we make decisions instead? How should we pick the right capex projects?"

Fredrik was quite surprised: he thought if they knew the problem, they would know the solution. But they'd never analyzed their capex decisions from a holistic point of view. Their conventional framework for capex analyses and planning certainly didn't help. As such, they didn't have the methods nor the tools to come up with an answer. SCA realized their need for a process change. Together with Erik Ottosson, who was then working at SCA, Fredrik went back to the drawing board, and they created the foundation for a new method as a response to management's question.

Over the past 25 years, Fredrik and Daniel have spent some 150,000 hours refining this approach, building on the solid foundation created with Ottosson—not to mention all the work carried out by our team and performed in conjunction with our clients—on identifying these situations, explaining them, developing tools for solving them, and working with clients to optimize their systems to maximize company cash flow.

Capitalizing on these opportunities has led to a sustained operating cash flow increase of at least 20% for our clients. While we would like to think that this is a testament to our expertise and insights, the truth is that the typical approach to capex has led companies badly astray over the past several decades. Our process simply corrects that.

Table 4.1 summarizes the differences between how capex is often practiced, versus how it should be practiced.

Table 4.1

|  | The Tail Wags the Dog | The Wiser Way to Capex |
| --- | --- | --- |
| Measure | payback, IRR, ROCE, NPV, etc. | company accumulated discounted cash flows |
| Process Focus | individual project analyses | entire production portfolio system |
| Time Perspective | going concern | creative destruction |
| Level of Perspective | tactical | strategic |

Because we approach capex from a systems viewpoint, we've been able to identify new opportunities in our clients' production portfolios. By our standards, we don't consider anything less than a 20% increase in current operating cash flow a successful capex strategy. More than once we've increased our clients' cash flows by 100%. Those are the kinds of opportunities hiding in plain sight, if you're looking through the right lens.

*Redesigning capex strategy is not a cost—it is the means to discover opportunities through better capital allocation.*

# PART II

# The Wiser Way to Capex

# THE STARTING
# BLOCK

At its heart, our holistic approach to capex allocation is straightforward. It doesn't require our proprietary software or specialized knowledge. In its simplest form, it can be done in Excel using nothing more complicated than the basic functions of adding, subtracting, multiplying, and dividing. Our process is the superior way to approach capex because it's built on systems thinking. It therefore completely avoids the issues described in previous chapters. We do not fix the issues because when we use our process, we never come across them.

Instead of viewing production as something a site does, we view production as something a network of sites does. Instead of seeing mills, plants, and factories as independent assets, we view them as tools to accomplish the aim of the system: sustainably maximizing company operating cash flow.

In the previous chapter, we gave a rudimentary example of systems thinking:

> For example, Quality Pulp could invest $100 million in a capex to expand capacity in Baton Rouge, but is that the best possible use of shareholder capital? What if the company instead

debottlenecked a production line in Albuquerque, invested in a new capability in one of their other B sites, consolidated Cleveland's capacity by adding two additional lines in another A site, and optimized all production lines? Would that be a better use of $100 million?

If Quality Pulp wants to add additional capacity, the viewpoint shouldn't be tactical: let's expand Baton Rouge. The viewpoint should be strategic: Does market demand justify increasing capacity? If so, what are all the possible ways we could increase production across our collection of sites (e.g., debottlenecking, adding production lines, consolidating production, adding capabilities, building a brownfield expansion, or even building a greenfield site)? Which combination of those possibilities—together with the benefits of funding the selected future replacement capex needs that will be spent—produces the greatest net cash flow (after capexes) and sustains that increase over the next 15 or 30 years? A small expansion? Several small expansions combined with closing the least competitive production? Or a large one in combination with one or two consolidations? How should the leadership at the helm of this company design the company's future?

That's a much more complex question involving calculations on the turnkey costs of each project, supply chain management optimization, freight costs, future market pricing and demand predictions, closure costs, sale of land, considering all replacement capex, accounting for exchange rates across countries, and the assessment of potentially hundreds of different combinations of those projects to find the single one that generates the highest cash flow. Since it is worth it, let's go to work! At the outset, it's important to understand the "who" and "how" of the capex strategy model being created.

## THE COMPANY TEAM

One of our core principles is to break down functional silos. To effectively create the kind of economic model required, those involved have to be the company's best and brightest. The project team must necessarily be cross functional; otherwise, it's simply not a holistic analysis. This team should include engineering, supply chain management, raw material procurement, controlling, marketing, and sales. Depending on the industry and company, the project team might also include experts in energy, sustainability, logistics, and so on.

The high-level steering team must be composed of the key executive managers from leadership. Experience has taught us that this team must absolutely include the CEO of the business; otherwise, the often-controversial findings will not be implemented, and no value will come from this process. In fact, the CEO should not want to be left out of the work where the future company is being designed—what else would the CEO be doing, if not that?

> ## Capex Strategy Keystone
> *Executive leadership must play an active role and the project team must be cross functional.*

Our method only works effectively with buy-in all around. Those who don't work with the economic model and its iterations during the project have a harder time understanding why some seemingly counterintuitive decisions make perfect sense, but only through the lens of the totality of the production system. Key personnel must be on the same page, singing the same tune, with the same confidence and conviction. The chosen capex strategy is the best out of all possible system alternatives. Everyone must agree the input data is sound and future assumptions are reasonable (not "correct," because there is no such thing when making assumptions about the future). They have to see how the economic model calculates cash flows to trust the outcome.

We encourage open, healthy discussions. Often, there are fierce debates. This is a necessary part of our method. Everyone must be able to challenge the model, its assumptions, its conclusions, and even industry conventions. This is the only way that, at the end of it all, everyone's ideas have been tested, all competing strategies have been evaluated, and the final course of action is obvious to everyone. While companies are not democracies and leadership, management, and the board will have the final say, these "free speech" debates and discussions are where the magic happens and where the best ideas come from. Management must welcome all discussions and all ideas, make sure all ideas are tested, and leave nothing and no one behind in the process.

In one project, the supply chain experts were emphatic that it wasn't feasible to ship raw materials more than 400 miles. Someone else on the team—someone who had nothing to do with procurement—said, "Are we sure that's true? Let's run the numbers." As it turned out, shipping costs did substantially increase under one strategy, but they were more than offset by the gains from the strategic alternative of consolidating three sites into one greenfield site, which dramatically lowered fixed costs. Despite more transportation-related emissions, the state-of-the-art facility significantly reduced $CO_2$ emissions, resulting in a substantial net reduction (and using substantially less water, too).

It is management's job to create an environment where ideas are applauded and even rewarded, even if they go against management's plans, expectations, and wishes. That is how you get to the best plan, and "best" is what management wants and needs as well as what shareholders demand. Not all company cultures or management individuals allow for this, though—which is unfortunate for everybody.

Our clients often include site managers in their project teams. In some instances, their economic model reveals their facility is like Cleveland: an aging site about to reach zero net cash flow. The benefit of having these site managers on the project team is not only for their contributions, but for their own sake. They have the opportunity to challenge the data, combine other strategic decisions, scrutinize outcomes, and consider a number of alternatives.

They come to the conclusion on their own that there really is no question about what's best for the business. They may not like it . . . but they accept it. Again and again, we've witnessed this.

## Potential Roles in the Three Levels of Contributors

**Leadership:** the high-level decision makers

- CEO, COO, and CFO
- Senior vice presidents of sales and marketing
- Senior vice presidents of supply chain and manufacturing
- Senior vice presidents of strategy

**Project Team:** the experts and best resources populating the economic model and simulating various combinations of strategic decisions, coming from functions such as:

- Supply and distribution
- Site management (optional)
- Engineering
- Controllers
- Energy consumption and production
- Sales and marketing
- Raw material procurement

**Local Teams (optional):** the people at the site-level who gather the raw data and information needed by the project team to create the basis of the economic model:

- Site manager
- Site engineer
- Heads of maintenance and production
- Site financial analyst

# THE DATA

For most companies, much of the data needed to model the economic interactions within the company's production portfolio doesn't yet exist, at least not digitally. By our methods, some of the data must be created by the project team, sometimes supported by the local teams.

We at Weissenrieder & Co. don't bring data to the model when we do projects with our clients: our clients' project teams do because they already have all the data and knowledge to create the analysis. They may not think they do, but they do, and it is always good enough since the future is so uncertain. We provide the philosophy, method, and experience, and we ensure the consistency of assumptions and guide the data collection and population—but all inputs, variables, and assumptions about future conditions come from the institutional knowledge and expertise within the company.

Our capex strategy projects are successful because the economic model and future projections result from company insiders creatively and collectively brainstorming. These insiders continually improve not only the model's data but various strategic decision combinations and how they are evaluated.

> ### Capex Strategy Keystone
> *The economic model is driven by the data created and collected by subject matter experts and is guided by executive leadership. This helps to create alignment around conclusions.*

# TIMELINE

Based on our experience over the past 25 years, we typically suggest allocating three calendar months for the six phases of such a project. There should be five leadership team meetings, signified with an "L" (kickoff, check-ins, and presentation of the recommendation for action). Figure 5.1 depicts this timeline, which encompasses asset mapping, project team meetings, and the project team's meeting with leadership.

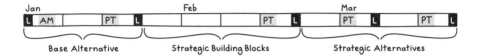

Within three weeks of kickoff, portions of the project team should have accomplished the asset mapping (AM) as well as the system's split of current EBITDA and its components into sites in a structure that allows for simulating various capex and business strategies. During this phase the project team may interact with local teams. Then the whole project team comes together over the course of two days, signified by "PT," to create the base alternative (BA). Everybody sits in the meeting, and future projections are inserted into the model live, in front of everyone. At the end of the first three weeks, they present the BA to leadership to discuss assumptions and outcomes.

In that same meeting, leadership and the project team list the first round of strategic building blocks (SBBs). These individual strategic capex decisions will later form the basis of various alternative capex strategies. Referring back to our Quality Pulp example, debottlenecking Albuquerque would be one SBB. Expanding Baton Rouge would be another SBB. The project team then spends the next three weeks collecting the requisite data related to all of those potential strategic initiatives.

After the data has been collected, the project team comes back together for a two-day meeting where team members share the data from the potential capexes and challenge each other's assumptions. Data is not inserted into the model before this meeting; it is done live, in front of the entire team. At the end of month two, the team convenes with leadership again to present the various SBBs, to be further challenged by executive management.

Within the next week, the project team assembles to run economic projections with various combinations of SBBs. Each combination of SBBs is called a strategic alternative (SA). Going back to our example once again: adding a substantial capacity increase at Baton Rouge while running the other two sites as in the base might be one SA. Deciding to debottleneck Albuquerque, add a new capability at a B site, and consolidating Cleveland's capacity by adding two new production lines at an A site would be a different SA. Both SAs might result in the additional capacity Quality Pulp wants, but one of them is going to generate a higher net cash flow than the other.

In the middle of month three, the project team meets again with leadership (still signified by "L" in Figure 5.1) to develop additional SAs the project team might not have considered, or with insights known only to leadership.

The following week, the project team meets one final time (still signified by "PT" in Figure 5.1) to discuss any further SAs, to select the most promising ones, and then subject those to sensitivity tests to see whether those SAs remain valid under different macroeconomic conditions. At the end of month three, the project team shares its recommendation for action (RfA) with leadership. The result: they have intentionally designed their company's future for the next 10 to 15 years.

## CONFLICTS IN SCOPE AND CONTROL

For most of our client engagements, the scope of the capex strategy project *is* the entire production system for the company, business, or division. There are exceptions to the rule, however. For example, we once worked with the packaging division of a pulp and paper company. The packaging division shared a mill with the pulp division. The site had two production lines—one devoted to pulp and the other to packaging. Managerially, these were two different lines of business, although they shared production assets.

Ideally, the economic model would have included the entire company. However, the pulp division wasn't prepared to commit the resources at that point. Operationally, it's impossible to have a model that encompasses only half a site since the conclusions can have an impact on the other half. As a consequence of that, since conclusions are drawn against the system, the impact is also on other pulp mills, never on individual mills. The maintenance teams, energy flows, and processes of the site were too intertwined to be split apart. The leadership of the packaging division made a case to corporate and was able to expand the scope of the project to include the entire scope of the interdependent divisions.

On the other hand, in some projects the scope of the capex strategy project included two or more production systems. This is especially common in integrated companies, such as a steel client that located its mill next to its ore mine. Although the mine supplied the mill with raw material, the two divisions could operate independently of each other, assuming market prices. In cases like these, we effectively create and run two economic models in parallel to one another.

Something similar happened with a client that had two production units in South America and two in Indonesia. Although all four sites produced the same products, for all intents and purposes they existed in two separate markets. For that industry, what happened in South America didn't really impact the market in Southeast Asia. Here again, we created two economic models and ran computer simulations independent of each other.

In another industry, our client had three sites in North America, two in China, and one in Malaysia—but they all functioned within the same market. A major production increase at one site would affect market price and supply opportunities for the other five. The scope of that economic model necessarily included all six sites.

There are two factors that should drive the scope of a capex strategy project: managerial control and interdependencies between the company's markets as well as between its production assets. The first factor may seem obvious: the economic model mainly encompasses what leadership has control over. (The things leadership doesn't control are addressed in the sensitivity analyses, covered in Chapter 11.) The combination of strategic decisions the project team considers during the project are necessarily ones the leadership can actually implement.

The second factor is the production assets' interdependencies. Economically, the iron mines and the mills could operate independently of each other. However, the pulp and packaging lines at the mill mentioned before could not. The two divisions shared infrastructure, energy solutions, maintenance personnel, and so forth. An effective economic model must include not only the assets under managerial control, but also the additional assets that depend on them to function or operate.

The same holds true for the client with six sites across two continents. In that industry, the market is global. Therefore, whatever happened at one site would affect the other five. The sites functioned as one interconnected production system.

## PRIMER ON ACCUMULATED DISCOUNTED CASH FLOWS AND CURVES

It's been our experience that the best way to literally see the differences between various capex strategies is to use a compelling visual. Our weapon of choice is accumulated discounted cash flow curves (or just "cash flow curves"). This metric isn't just a powerful graph but one that allows the team to instantly understand the costs and benefits of one collection of capital allocation decision chains against another, useful in the short, medium, and long term. It allows the team to quickly track the momentum of cash flows over the time period considered. It's an important tool that lets the team quickly answer such questions as: Are we adding value by increasing our competitiveness and long-term sustainability? Are we merely "harvesting" value at this point? Are we investing a substantial amount of time and resources but in return for gaining little ground? Should we invest a little to get a little or invest a lot to gain much more?

As we've discussed, one-dimensional metrics—NPV, payback, IRR, and so on—are the go-to metrics for typical capex analyses of individual projects (but they're fundamentally the wrong tools for the job). In the context of cash flow curves, those metrics also fall short because they're insufficient when ranking full-scale capex strategies against each other: they lack the ability to capture how a capex strategy reaches a certain value over time.

To explain accumulated discounted cash flow curves, let's use yet another fictional company; this time, Really Big Steel. The company projects that its production portfolio will earn $100 a year over the next 10 years, shown simply in Table 5.1.

**Table 5.1**

| Year | 0 | 1 | 2 | 3 | 4 | 5 | 6 | 7 | 8 | 9 | 10 |
|---|---|---|---|---|---|---|---|---|---|---|---|
| Cash Flow After Capexes per Year | – | 100 | 100 | 100 | 100 | 100 | 100 | 100 | 100 | 100 | 100 |

If we were to graph this, we'd get a straightforward line as shown in Figure 5.2.

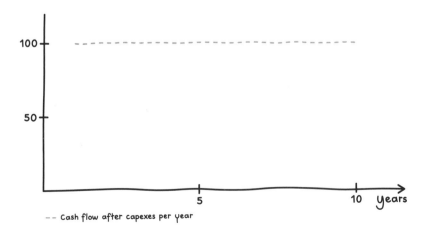

-- Cash flow after capexes per year

Let's first look at accumulated cash flows. That is, each year's cash flow gets added to all the ones before it. Again, in a simple table, it looks like Table 5.2.

**Table 5.2**

| Year | 0 | 1 | 2 | 3 | 4 | 5 | 6 | 7 | 8 | 9 | 10 |
|---|---|---|---|---|---|---|---|---|---|---|---|
| Cash Flow After Capexes per Year | – | $100 | $100 | $100 | $100 | $100 | $100 | $100 | $100 | $100 | $100 |
| Accumulated Cash Flow | $0 | $100 | $200 | $300 | $400 | $500 | $600 | $700 | $800 | $900 | $1,000 |

We start from zero. In year one, Really Big Steel earns $100. In year two, it earns another $100. So by year two, the company has accumulated $200 in cash flows so far. In year three, it earns another $100. Added to the previous year's accumulated cash flows, it yields a total of $300 in accumulated cash flows, and so on.

Graphing these accumulated cash flows results in Figure 5.3.

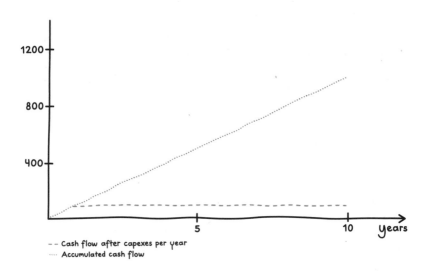

Now, we have to talk about risk and the time value of money. It could be summarized in the old saying, "A bird in hand is worth two in the bush." Meaning, possessing something for sure today is worth more than the promise of earning even more tomorrow. There's a certain risk that comes with gambling on the future, and companies need to account for that risk. The way they do so is by "discounting" the value of the future money.

Really Big Steel is considered a risky investment. For the company's owners, $100 next year is only worth $83 to them today. In year two, the company will earn another $100, but from the owners' point of view, they only believe that much cash to be worth $69 in today's money. Each year, $100 is worth less and less than it is today—that is, from the time of their analysis.

Really Big Steel arrived at those numbers by using a discount rate of 20% each year, the company's assumed WACC. (Normally, 20% is too high for a capital cost to be realistic. We use it here to make the explanation and graphs easier to grasp.) The $100 of cash flow next year is discounted using 20% to get to today's value of money reflecting both risk and inflation (or $83). The $100 of cash flow in year two is discounted two years using a 20% discount rate (or $69). In year three, that cash flow is discounted an additional year using 20%. By the end of the decade, $100 is only worth $16 today to Really Big Steel's owners.

This is shown in Table 5.3.

Table 5.3

| Year | 0 | 1 | 2 | 3 | 4 | 5 | 6 | 7 | 8 | 9 | 10 |
|---|---|---|---|---|---|---|---|---|---|---|---|
| Discounted Cash Flow After Capexes per Year | $0 | $83 | $69 | $58 | $48 | $40 | $33 | $28 | $23 | $19 | $16 |

These are the real numbers Really Big Steel is after. How much *value* do its future cash flows deliver in today's dollars?

Similar to how we accumulated cash flows before, we do so again. Only this time, we're not adding a year's cash flow to all the previous years' cash flows—we're adding the *value* of each year's cash flow (in today's dollars) to the cash flows of all the years that came before.

If year one's cash flow is only worth $83 today and year two's cash flow is only worth $69, then the accumulated cash flow in year two is $83 + $69.

Running those calculations yields Table 5.4.

**Table 5.4**

| Year | 0 | 1 | 2 | 3 | 4 | 5 | 6 | 7 | 8 | 9 | 10 |
|---|---|---|---|---|---|---|---|---|---|---|---|
| Cash Flow After Capexes per Year | – | $100 | $100 | $100 | $100 | $100 | $100 | $100 | $100 | $100 | $100 |
| Accumulated Cash Flow | $0 | $100 | $200 | $300 | $400 | $500 | $600 | $700 | $800 | $900 | $1,000 |

| | 0 | 1 | 2 | 3 | 4 | 5 | 6 | 7 | 8 | 9 | 10 |
|---|---|---|---|---|---|---|---|---|---|---|---|
| Discounted Cash Flow After Capexes per Year | $0 | $83 | $69 | $58 | $48 | $40 | $33 | $28 | $23 | $19 | $16 |
| Accumulated Discounted Cash Flows | $0 | $83 | $153 | $211 | $259 | $299 | $333 | $360 | $384 | $403 | $419 |

Over the next 10 years, Really Big Steel's production portfolio will deliver $419 in total value (again, as measured in today's money).

Combining the accumulated discounted cash flows with Figure 5.3 yields Figure 5.4.

Before discounting the company's cash flows each year, its accumulated cash flows graphed as a nice diagonal line. Due to discounting each year's worth, however, the graph of its accumulated cash flows bends slightly. We use the word "slightly," but visually the result is a cash flow curve much less exciting than the curve that accumulated but didn't discount.

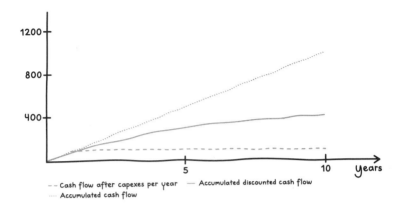

1200

800

400

5          10     years

-- Cash flow after capexes per year  — Accumulated discounted cash flow
···· Accumulated cash flow

Of course, earning the exact same cash flow year after year isn't realistic. When we work with a client to create a capex strategy model and then graph its accumulated discounted cash flows (which we call the base alternative), the curve more often looks like Figure 5.5.

### Accumulated discounted cash flow

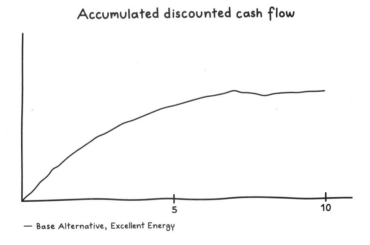

5                              10

— Base Alternative, Excellent Energy

We've removed the $y$ axis cash values because, for the purposes of understanding what this cash flow curve means, the actual numbers don't matter. More importantly, the numbers will be wrong anyway. Future cash flows are, by their very nature, about an uncertain future. Any cash flow projections are made on assumptions;

we know that those assumptions will be wrong, sometimes terribly wrong. When it comes to alternative capex strategies, the curves' actual numbers don't matter; what matters is how they graph in relation to each other.

Let's say this, in fact, is the cash flow curve for another company. Let's call it Excellent Energy. The curve starts at time and cash flow of zero because we only include future cash flow. By trending upward, it shows Excellent Energy enjoying positive discounted cash flows, right up until year seven. In year eight, the curve dips. This means there was negative cash flow in year eight (perhaps due to a large capital expenditure). However, the curve immediately begins trending upward again in years 9 and 10. The company's cash flows were once again positive in these years.

However, the curve flattens out in those last two years. This signifies that the production portfolio is no longer adding additional value to Excellent Energy. It has reached its maximum accumulated discounted cash flow for the base alternative; the company cash flow is around zero. That is, unless leadership decides to do something different, perhaps such as adding a new production line that generates higher cash flows (which we would call strategic alternative one).

If that were the case, the new cash flow curve might look like Figure 5.6.

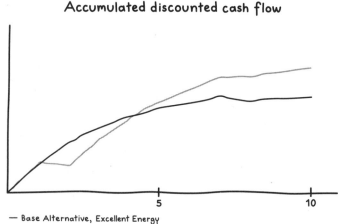

## Accumulated discounted cash flow

— Base Alternative, Excellent Energy
— SA1

Here, we can see when the company spent the money for the new production line in year two where the curve dips. It won't be until year four that this potential strategic alternative matches the accumulated discounted cash flows of just keeping things as they are. But thereafter, for years 5 through 10, not only is the new cash flow curve of SA1 greater than the base alternative, it trends upward, indicating a continual increase in value to the company each year. From a sustainability point of view, the alternative is clearly superior to going by the base alternative.

In fact, while the base alternative's curve begins to flatten out by year nine, the strategic alternative's curve looks like it will continue to rise. In a standard analysis, we would go far beyond 10 years for our analysis. We use long time horizons—longer than anybody on our clients' teams thinks is relevant, because redesigning an enterprise takes time. A large restructuring capex strategy in some industries can take up to 10 years. Then the discounted payback of that restructuring might be 8 to 10 years. Then we'd want to see how the system develops after that (at least compared with other options) for, let's say, a decade. That pushes the time horizon up toward 30 years.

A convenient feature of these cash flow curves is that each person can focus on the time horizon relevant to him or her. The CFO might be interested in only the first five years so she can consider how to finance the capex strategy. The CEO and COO, on the other hand, might look at 20 years, since they evaluate various strategic alternatives' discounted paybacks against each other, as well as the company's long term development and competitiveness.

Lastly, let's talk about delta cash flow curves, or simply "delta curves" (not to be confused with the delta calculations we discussed earlier). A delta curve is a complement to the ordinary curves, but must never be used as a substitute. For instance, delta curves are used when a situation needs to be highlighted better, or when the resolution of a curve/situation needs to increase. A delta curve basically flattens out one curve and makes it the $x$ axis. Then, it graphs the second curve relative to the first. The graph of the second curve will show the difference between the original two curves.

Let's say the company's base alternative's discounted cash flow curve was the *x* axis. How does the alternative perform in relation to the base? Graphing that out produces Figure 5.7.

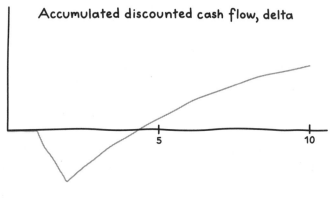

Accumulated discounted cash flow, delta

— Delta Base and SA1, Excellent Energy

As we discussed, the base alternative and strategic alternative 1 have the same cash flow in year one. In this graph, that's why the curve overlays the *x* axis for the first year. In year two of strategic alternative one, there is a major outlay of cash while the new production line is being installed. We can see that the capital expenditure reaches a discounted payback against the base alternative in year four.

But just like their evil delta calculation cousins, delta curves can be deceiving. To illustrate what we mean, Figure 5.8 shows the accumulated discounted cash flow curve for a completely new company, Grand Agriculture, that has only one site.

We can see that Grand Agriculture's production reaches its peak value at year four. In year five, there is a major capex replacement project required to keep the site running. That's why the cash flows turn negative that year. The site's cash flow never recovers to its earlier levels.

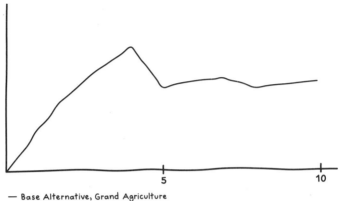

Accumulated discounted cash flow

— Base Alternative, Grand Agriculture

Let's say this company's leadership plans to expand the site. In year two, leadership decides to allocate the capital for this expansion project. After charting the cash flows, the updated graph is shown in Figure 5.9.

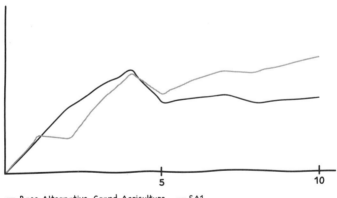

Accumulated discounted cash flow

— Base Alternative, Grand Agriculture    — SA1

The choice to expand will lower this site's cash flow initially due to the investment outlay. The large capital expenditure in year five is still needed, so the strategic alternative's curve reflects that by dipping during year five. After that, however, the curve trends upward. Clearly, this is the better choice of the two, but is it the *best* choice out of *all* possible options?

Well, we know that in Grand Agriculture's base alternative, the big capex replacement project in year five effectively killed its site from adding any further value, so why do it at all? What if, instead, its leadership looked at the results of simply running the site for cash and closing it when the large year five replacement need appears?

Figure 5.10 depicts this scenario.

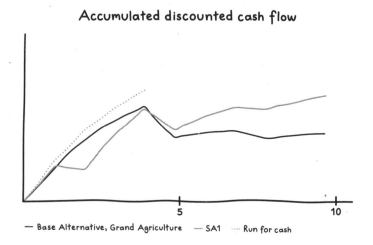

Accumulated discounted cash flow

— Base Alternative, Grand Agriculture    — SA1    ⋯⋯ Run for cash

The company value would peak in year four. Since that's how its production system can provide the maximum amount of shareholder value, Grand Agriculture's leadership decides to pursue this radical yet justified course of action. The company runs the site for cash and then closes it after four years.

Now, let's return to our discussion on delta curves. If we were to make Grand Agriculture's base alternative cash flow curve the *x* axis and then compare the first strategic alternative (that included the expansion capex as well as the major replacement capex) to it, management would see the graph in Figure 5.11.

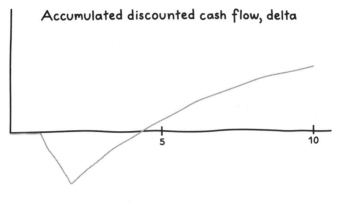

Accumulated discounted cash flow, delta

5   10

— Delta Base and SA1, Grand Agriculture

Grand Agriculture's delta curve looks exactly like Excellent Energy's, despite the different contexts and cash flows. The same discounted payback at the same time with the same present value in year 10. Yet in Excellent Energy's case, its first alternative yields its maximum value. For Grand Agriculture, the exact same graph doesn't.

This is why we don't use delta curves as more than a complementary tool, only for certain situations: they don't provide the full picture.

## SUMMARY

We have found that visualizing strategies' cash flow is powerful. To summarize:

- Evaluate and compare capex plans by using accumulated discounted cash flow curves that represent the entire production system.
- Aim to get the cash flow curve for the entire system as high as possible at an acceptable risk.
- Cash flow curves allow for effective short-, medium-, and long-term analyses.

- The absolute numbers for future projections will be wrong; the purpose of the curves is to compare which one yields the best position.
- Delta curves aren't sufficient to analyze a holistic capex strategy.
- Cash flow curves are powerful visual storytelling tools.

With the project composition, management, and administration issues addressed, we turn to understanding the workings of the economic model. The approach we're about to present runs counter to nearly everything we all have learned about capex analysis.

# 6

# CREATING A CAPEX STRATEGY MODEL

The purpose of creating an economic model is to enable whole-business capex strategy analyses, with many simulations and sensitivity analyses. To create the economic model that encompasses a company's entire production system requires six major phases:

1. Asset mapping for the base alternative (BA)
2. Cash flows for the BA
3. Strategic building blocks (SBBs)
4. Strategic alternatives (SAs)
5. Sensitivity tests
6. Recommendation for action (RfA)

The whole process is illustrated in Figure 6.1.

The first step is to create the BA. The BA is an analytical starting point modeling the current system's ability to generate cash flow. It is a tool we use to consistently and effectively be able to later create numerous strategic building blocks (SBBs) and strategic alternatives (SAs) and compare them in a relevant way. The BA is the basis for the capex strategy model, as well as a database for a lot of data on volumes, capacities, capex needs, and so on.

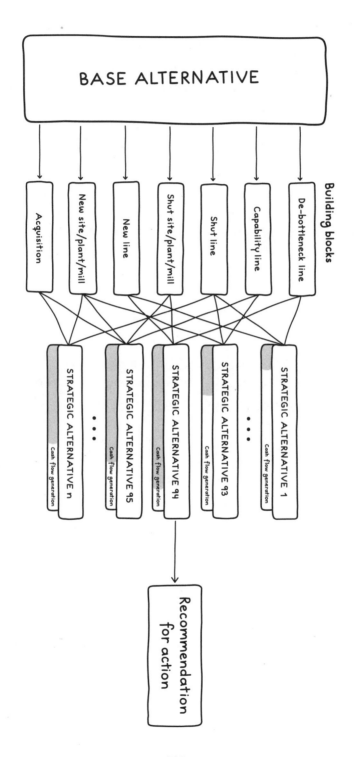

BASE ALTERNATIVE

Building blocks

Acquisition

New site/plant/mill

New line

Shut site/plant/mill

Shut line

Capability line

De-bottleneck line

STRATEGIC ALTERNATIVE n    Cash flow generation

STRATEGIC ALTERNATIVE 95    Cash flow generation

STRATEGIC ALTERNATIVE 94    Cash flow generation

STRATEGIC ALTERNATIVE 93    Cash flow generation

STRATEGIC ALTERNATIVE 1    Cash flow generation

Recommendation for action

While we call the base alternative an alternative, it's not necessarily a realistic one since it's based strictly on the going concern principle. Its purpose is not to reflect a current capex strategy, quite the opposite. The baseline reference is essentially the "pre-strategy" or "only legacy strategy" capex plan, like putting an airplane on autopilot: What do we need to do to maintain current course, speed, and altitude? That means there is no new strategic intent beyond what is reflected in the legacy footprint from this point forward. While the BA is not an alternative we recommend,* its purpose is to provide a consistent starting point when creating SBBs and SAs and to serve as a baseline for comparison with the yet-to-be-created SAs. It is the fixed reference point that capex delta calculations lack. When the project team starts creating strategic alternatives to the baseline, it has to have an absolute reference to compare each SA's cash flow to.

In some industries and markets, a five-year capital allocation strategy makes sense. In others, it might take 5 or, in the case of nuclear power plants, 15 years to even implement one strategic decision, much less begin reaping the benefits. We've never created a capex strategy model that covered anything less than a 20-year time span.† Typically, clients' capex strategy models cover more like 30 years. It depends on what's important to the capex team. We run the model beyond the time horizon anyone would be interested in looking at. For our particular clients, that's often 30-plus years.

To explain our process first at a high level, we're going to use another hypothetical company: Superior Paper, GmbH, headquartered in Luxembourg. The company has four paper mills scattered across Europe. The company's youngest one sits on the outskirts of North London. The company's oldest mill is in Helsinki, Finland.

---

* Theoretically, there might be cases where we would. We use it for parts of systems.

† The actual recommendation for action, however, usually covers a 5- to 10-year period but is based on a 30-year analysis. We do not recommend, for example, converting a machine 15 years into the future, but we would analyze how a system with a converted machine 5 years out would most likely perform 20 years later.

Because of its aged technology, Helsinki has some quality issues; the company can only sell a portion of its total capacity. Then there are its two mills that fall somewhere in between. One is in Brussels, Belgium, while the other is in Frankfurt, Germany. After Superior Paper's project team creates the BA modeling the production cash flows of the four mills, it finds the accumulated discounted cash flow curve in Figure. 6.2.

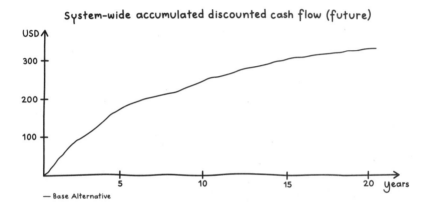

The upward slope of the curve is a good sign. We typically see the curve peak at some point in the BA (that is where the cash flow goes negative) usually 15 to 20 years out. The worst baseline we have seen peaked after just two years in the BA and then went straight down into the basement. Thankfully, it wasn't too late to turn that company around.

With Superior Paper's current portfolio, cash flows will continue to be positive and accumulate year after year for the next 20 years, even if the company does nothing but invest in the necessary and required capexes to maintain operations. With that curve as the baseline reference, once the SBBs are developed and the team begins to combine them, the team can compare the cash flows of different SAs before ultimately arriving at the RfA.

One possible strategic combination might be to close the facility in London and debottleneck Frankfurt, resulting in a capacity increase at that site by 100 units. In our example, this is their eighth combination of SBBs. As such, we would call it SA8. After running Superior Paper's capex strategy model with those inputs, the team finds the value curve in Figure 6.3.

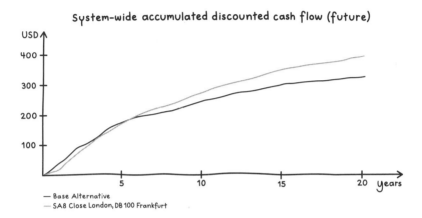

This graph shows two different possible futures. One where the company only funds the four sites' essential capex needs (the BA) and the other where Superior Paper stops production in London and debottlenecks the Frankfurt mill (SA8). In SA8, after the initial spend on the debottlenecking capex in Frankfurt (net the proceeds of closing the London operations and selling the land), the system increases its cash flow and reaches a discounted payback in year six. After six years, SA8 continues to generate more cash flow than the BA does. Clearly, SA8 is the superior choice.

But does SA8 produce the *maximum* cash flow Superior Paper's production system is capable of? The only way to know is to continually create different combinations of capex projects and then graph their accumulated discounted cash flow curves. While we've simplified the number to considering just a handful of SAs for this example, in reality teams go through dozens or hundreds of iterations in search of the strategic choices that will lead to highest possible cash flow over the next 20 to 30 years.

But these cash flow projections are only as good as the economic model that produced them. The underpinnings of the model are absolutely critical to an effective capex strategy. That's why this chapter is devoted to the assumptions the model is based on.

> ## Capex Strategy Keystone
>
> *Complete the entire economic model and the base alternative before creating any strategic building blocks or alternatives.*

In our process, the BA rests on the following assumptions:

1. There is no strategic intent going forward. The base alternative is composed of the essential capexes required to maintain the company's ability to technically keep serving today's customers using its existing asset footprint.
2. All production sites are treated equally. There is no preferential treatment among the sites such as expecting one will be closed.
3. Each site will continue to produce its current product mix serving its current customer base. Quality driven capex might be needed for the future in the base alternative to accomplish this.
4. We assume that environmental regulations and safety standards will level up. Consequently, future unseen capexes will be needed and must be accounted for.
5. Absent a strategic response to market forces, the sites' EBITDA margins will decline and, as a result, the company's overall EBITDA margins will decline.
6. System interactions are calculated according to market prices, regardless of company practices.

# The Capex Strategy Model at a Glance

The purpose of our process is to create a practical, calculative, dynamic, predictive, long-term enterprisewide capital allocation strategy assessment simulator. Unlike Billy Beane and baseball's sabermetrics experts, our method requires zero statistics. Simply add, subtract, multiply, and divide. With the right team, any company can create its own. To break down this rather lengthy description:

- **Practical:** While grounded in academic theory, our process was created in the trenches and grounded in reality to provide an analytical tool for executives. It accounts for business needs, customer demands, currency fluctuations, market changes, and other factors outside of executives' control.
- **Calculative:** We've seen executives talk about capex strategy in vague generalities. Because our method uses cold, hard numbers, it allows our clients to measure the results of different strategies in cold, hard cash. This method literally calculates strategy. The best company strategy comes as a result of data input and mathematical functions, not abstract and unquantified assumptions.
- **Dynamic:** A static, one-time model that captured a company's production system as it exists today would be useful in and of itself. Our process, on the other hand, allows executives to endlessly change variables (choosing one strategy over another, seeing what would happen if a great recession- or Covid-like event were to happen, etc.) and instantly get the results calculated down to the cent.
- **Predictive:** Technically, our process does something better than predict how different decisions will play out over years—it projects what will happen. Truly,

there is often little guesswork. With a thorough data collection process (from institutional knowledge, financial statements, internal estimates, and more) and the ability to subject simulations to various market conditions, our process allows leadership to confidently chart a path forward.

- **Long term:** The purpose of our method isn't to create a capex plan for the upcoming year. Our clients routinely use it to create a capex strategy for the next 5 to 10 years and then derive a long-term, actionable capex plan based on the greater strategy.
- **Strategy:** Today, capex is essentially a bottom-up approach. Site managers submit capex requests; executives choose between the best options. This is what we call "the tail wags the dog" since the capex strategy is then a consequence of the tactically chosen capex projects, an unconscious action. Our method, on the other hand, is a systems-based approach. That means focusing on the larger decisions and creating the best possible company from a systems point of view.
- **Assessment:** The capex strategy model is a tool that allows executives to put a dollar sign next to each potential strategy. We once had a client that kept one barely functional site operating because it served one of the company's biggest and oldest clients. That's a strategic decision. Our client's capex model, however, allowed it to compare the costs of keeping the site (and the ensuing customer) versus shuttering it and investing those resources elsewhere. In this case, the cost to keep the one customer turned out to be staggering.

# ASSUMPTION 1: NO STRATEGIC INTENT

The base alternative is a "pure" analytical tool. It's not created to model a realistic or desired future. This is a fundamental rule of the BA. It is simply the output of an economic model that captures the company's production system as it stands today and then projects the output into the future. It is the continuation of today's production in perpetuity. There are no plans for any expansions, closures, acquisitions, or anything strategic of the sort. Put another way, the capex plan from the BA will be the answer to the question: What's the least we have to do to maintain our current production footprint and customers in the long term?

The BA identifies the baseline capital need, the capital expenditures that are actually needed in the long term to defend a given footprint of production units. The baseline capex need is often a lot larger than executives first expect. Anchoring to historic capex levels and depreciation levels are usually the culprit for those false expectations.

# ASSUMPTION 2: NO SPECIAL TREATMENT

More than once we've worked with clients that assign their worst product runs to their best sites. Why? "Because that's the only mill that can run it without losing money," we've heard. In other cases, they'll arbitrarily assign product runs to certain plants "because, otherwise, it won't have anything to run."

Because the BA assumes no further strategic intent—that all sites and products are treated homogeneously—our process disallows manipulating elements and interactions within the system to achieve such desired outcomes. Usually, such issues don't crop up until the team begins running different SAs.

*So often, we hear people say, "Oh, that's not how we do capex in our company," or our favorite, "Our problems are different." The details may vary, but the fundamentals are the same and the solution is the same. That's why our approach to capex strategy is universal in nature.*

# ASSUMPTION 3: KEEP PRODUCTION AS IS

The BA assumes that each site's existing product mix will continue serving its existing market. As such, the BA assumes the board will approve the base capital necessary to do so. Production assets won't be improved beyond what's necessary to keep up with quality expectations from customers. Aside from that, there will be no additional product capabilities, conversions, and so on. It is assumed that the company will fund the capexes necessary to remain as competitive as it is today. These include normal wear and tear, replacements, refurbishments, and more. The BA treats these as necessary and assumes they will be implemented. It doesn't matter what these capex projects cost, nor how practical they might be. A site might be 60 years old and the company believes it's nearing the end of its life cycle. It doesn't matter—the BA treats this site as if it will produce forever.

With Superior Paper's mill in London, for instance, an excerpt of the necessary capexes (in simplified figures) over the next 20 years might be look like Table 6.1.

Table 6.1

| London | Year 1 | Year 2 | Year 3 | Year 5 | Year 8 | Year 10 | Year 11 | Year 20 |
|---|---|---|---|---|---|---|---|---|
| Capex Outlays | –$5 | –$3 | –$9 | –$11 | –$10 | –$4 | –$9 | –$4 |

As with our prior example of Quality Pulp Manufacturing, these numbers could represent thousands or hundreds of millions of dollars. The scale is immaterial.

# ASSUMPTION 4: CAPEX NEEDS WILL GROW

Beyond the capexes required to maintain operations, the BA will typically also assume that the costs of meeting environmental regulations and safety standards will continue to rise. In addition to the known capexes already required, the BA assumes there will be additional capexes as new legislation is introduced, especially in certain industries with rapidly evolving environmental regulations. In the example of Superior Paper, we assume the cumulative effect of those new regulations and standards will be $5 every five years per mill. While the company may not be able to specify what those required capex projects will be today, it does know those projects will arise.

Customers' quality expectations will continue to rise. The BA needs to compensate for this. If a company knows a facility is behind on quality, or soon will be, then that needs to be fixed in the BA.

# ASSUMPTION 5: EBITDA MARGINS WILL DECLINE

The BA assumes no strategic intent and a steady relative market position, which means the BA does *not* respond to major changes in technology, and against competitors. It does, however, assume that the world will continue to turn. Competitors will adopt the latest technologies. Customers' demands will evolve. The twin forces of creative destruction—rising costs and falling prices, as discussed in Chapter 3—squeeze the EBITDA margins in the BA. There's no strategic response to counter it in the BA. The EBITDA margin squeeze is not unique to our process: it's a fundamental assumption that must go into all financial planning and analysis to avoid unfounded optimism. The effect is the company's EBITDA margins in the BA will steadily decline. (If the margins don't decline, the team has incorrectly set up the BA.)

> Labor was the first price, the original purchase—money that was paid for all things. It was not by gold or by silver, but by labor, that all wealth of the world was originally purchased.
>
> —Adam Smith

Technically, strictly following the BA would result in a company's demise as the gap between its competitiveness and its peers' widens. In fact, something like this happens in the free market every day: companies that fail to respond to market changes (or respond in an incorrect way) on a strategic level continue to lose their competitive edge and eventually go out of business.

To be more specific, when projecting the economic model's future cash flows, the team must consider—and plan for—market forces as follows:

- In the long term, market prices for land and labor will rise faster than inflation.
- In the long term, the inflation in market prices for intermediary or finished goods will not be able to keep up with the inflation in the input variables such as labor and raw material.

Individual companies might have stable or, even for a couple of years, increasing EBITDA margins in a BA due to the cycle. An industry as a whole is, over time, still subject to market forces. The costs of nonrenewable inputs—land, timber, and iron ore, for example—as well as labor costs rise over time, even accounting for inflation. The prices of goods and services produced, such as computers, cloud services, and renewable energy sources—solar and wind—are likely to decline in real terms over time because of efficiency gains in technology and methods. Thus, the EBITDA margins in Superior Paper's BA will show a decrease at the site level as shown in Figure 6.4.

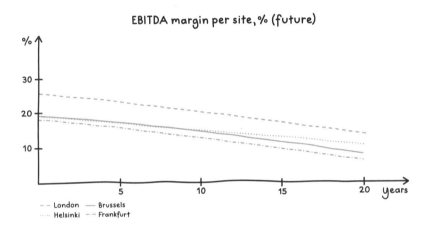

And a decrease at the aggregate level as seen in Figure 6.5.

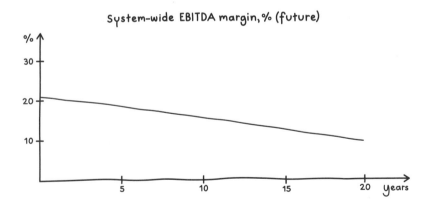

After developing the BA, the team at Superior Paper notes that London's EBITDA margin is clearly the best of the four. Perhaps surprisingly, the old mill at Helsinki is second. Really, though, these graphs don't offer any insights into which potential capex strategies would be best.

# ASSUMPTION 6: MARKET-BASED INTERNAL PRICING

As much as possible, we strongly encourage companies to use market-based internal pricing, regardless of company policy. Earlier, we talked about how sawmills are often treated as simply part of the mill's supply chain; the same can be true for iron ore mines. In these cases, our clients used cost-based transfer pricing to procure their pulp mills' or steel mills' raw material. In building the BA, we advised the teams to ignore the cost-based transfer pricing and use market prices for the internally transferred wood chips and ore instead.*

In another project, we worked with the agricultural division in a vertically integrated food company. Leadership was unable to expand the scope of its capex strategy project to include the downstream divisions such as produce conversion, packaging, and canning. Normally, this wouldn't be an issue. As indicated earlier, in our process, the team would build the economic model as if the division were a stand-alone business. Unlike the iron mines, though, the parent company would not allow the agricultural division to supply the open market. The division was mandated to exclusively supply downstream operations and to do so on a cost-based transfer price. In general, we follow Dr. W. Edwards Deming's advice: "The obligation of any component is to contribute its best to the system, not to maximize its own production, profit, or sales, nor any other competitive measure. Some components may operate at a loss to themselves in order to optimize the

---

* This is valuable to do even when there is a "true" market failure (i.e., where there, in practice, is not a reasonable way to go to the market).

whole system. . . . "* However, when the scope of the project is limited, a team has no choice but to seek to optimize its own division. And one must use market pricing to understand where value is created and where it is not, if it is more valuable to source raw material externally than internally, and so on.

Fortunately, those limitations don't change the effectiveness of our approach. We still used market-based transfer pricing in the capex strategy model. As a result, the company could demonstrate to its parent company how much value (in cost savings) the upstream division provided *and* how much the company was losing by disallowing it to serve the free market.

That's a powerful story.

• • •

With a basic grasp of the base alternative, we can begin going through each phase of our process, beginning with strategic asset mapping in the next chapter.

---

* Deming, W. Edwards. *The New Economics for Industry, Government, Education, Third Edition*. Cambridge, MA: MIT Press, 2018.

# THE BASE
# ALTERNATIVE:
# STRATEGIC ASSET
# MAPPING

In *Thinking in Systems*, Donella Meadows wrote, "A system is more than the sum of its parts. A system isn't just any old collection of things. A system is an interconnected set of elements that is coherently organized in a way that achieves something . . . a system [consists] of three kinds of things: elements, interconnections, and a function or purpose."* For the company's production system, the team must identify its purpose, its elements, and the interactions between those elements. We've already stated the purpose of the system (to sustainably increase accumulated discounted cash flow). In this phase of our process, a portion of the team identifies the elements of the system: the production assets in play. That is, the actual equipment, aka the capital.

---

* Meadows, DH. *Thinking in Systems: A Primer.* White River Junction, VT: Chelsea Green Publishing Company. 2008.

The engineering resources in the project team begin by listing all the production sites in the portfolio. Within those sites, all the major production assets, equipment, machinery, and other assets above a certain threshold are listed. For our industrial clients, these are usually assets with a capex replacement cost of at least $1 million. (Our process scales to any size of operations. In a company with a small industrial facility, $50,000 might be a sizable capex.) For each of those identified assets, the team must answer four key questions:

1. What is its operational age?
2. What is the turnkey cost to replace/refurbish it today?
3. What is its current useful life?
4. In general, what is this asset's standard useful life?

---

### Capex Strategy Keystone

*The project team must create original strategic asset mapping data.*

---

# QUESTION 1.
# OPERATIONAL AGE

The team needs to know the asset's age. Not its literal age, but from the perspective of its technical age. We used to ask, "When was it built?" but that would often lead to the team pulling the original installment date. From a production point of view, these "balance sheet dates" don't matter. Its original installment date doesn't say how long the asset has actually been in operation as seen from a technical age view. If a production line has been rebuilt, then the original date of installation is irrelevant. For all practical purposes, being rebuilt resets (or at least partially resets) the clock on assets.

What the team needs is a practical approximation of the technical age of the equipment. Because capital-intensive equipment is often complex, it happens that just a significant part of an asset has been replaced. More often than not, the asset has been replaced piecemeal with multiple components at various technical ages. In those cases, the team calculates a reasonable approximate age. From a practical viewpoint, though, exact accuracy isn't necessary. Three years within its true weighted average startup date is usually sufficient for the capex strategy model. If the asset is more than 20 years old the start-up date can be even less accurate.

# QUESTION 2.
# REPLACEMENT COST NEW

Next, the team asks what it would cost to replace the asset with its modern equivalent. As part of the BA, this means producing the same outputs at the same capacity. By "cost" we mean the total turnkey costs, including engineering and installation.

We've never encountered a company that does not have the right people with the knowledge to create this original asset data. At the same time, we have also never encountered a company with these numbers readily available in a ledger or database. In fact, readily available numbers are suspect because they're often derived from deflated historic accounting data—not updated current costs— and are not at all structured to provide the structure needed for capex strategy. Here, accounting ledgers for example are more misleading than revealing. Companies often have asset ledgers, but the data doesn't pertain to production or current replacement costs and especially does not consider technological developments and the oftentimes substantial inflation of components, engineering costs, and so on.

### Data Shortcuts

Managers sometimes want to shortcut creating original data in the asset mapping phase. They ask: "Why reinvent the wheel? Why can't we just use the data we have?" We respond with the following story.

The legendary Madison Avenue advertising executive David Ogilvy used to tell the story about a man walking home one night and passing someone obviously looking for something lost by the light of a streetlight.

The passerby said, "Sir, is there something I can help you find?"

The man said, "Yes, please! I'm afraid I've lost my keys."

Being a Good Samaritan, the passerby said, "Well, let me help you." He searched all around the lamppost as far as the light would reach. After a fruitless search, he finally said, "Sir, are you sure this is where you lost your keys?"

"What? Oh, no, I lost them over there in the dark."

Quite confused, the Good Samaritan asked, "Then why on Earth are you looking over here by the lamppost?"

He said, "Because this is where the light is."

The moral of the story: you shouldn't use readily available data just because it's easy to find. To find what you're really looking for, you must sometimes look where there is no light. When the data needed can't be found, it must be created. This means the team must estimate these costs, relying on its expertise, best guesses, and whatever information it can cobble together.

With larger equipment, it's often the case that a component of it can be replaced by itself, and the remainder can be replaced later. If this component's replacement cost meets the set threshold amount, the team can treat the component as a stand-alone asset and break it out from the larger equipment. In the economic model, the cost of replacing the larger asset is divided into two parts: the cost to replace the component and the remaining costs to replace the rest of the asset. For instance, if a company's chosen threshold amount is $500,000, then an asset costing $2,750,000 to replace might be broken down into a $750,000 component and $2,000,000 for the rest of the asset. The component may be replaced 3 years from now while the rest of the asset is replaced 10 years after that.

# QUESTION 3.
# USEFUL LIFE

This topic could be stated as: How much longer can we expect this asset to last before it needs to be replaced, given the definition of the base alternative (BA)? How much more time can the team expect it to remain in operation if the team is still to comply with safety and environmental standards as well as customer demands? How long will it last from an aging point of view and when would this asset typically be replaced if this were a going concern entity? When will the asset require a capital expenditure to keep it in running order? Here, we suggest accuracy to be within a year (at least for the first five years of the projected future). After that period, accuracy quickly deteriorates for obvious reasons.

# QUESTION 4.
# STANDARD USEFUL LIFE

In the first five years, the team should be able to determine how much useful life a current piece of equipment has remaining. But the further past that point the projections go, the more the team has to rely on the standard useful life of such assets in general. Put another way, the team wants to know: When will the company have to make another capex investment to replace this asset or component again? If the team is creating a BA that goes 30 years into the future, it's critical that the team know if a particular asset is likely to be replaced every decade. If so, the BA has to account for that capex every 10 years. At the same time, for many of our clients at least, the majority of a site's assets do not need to be replaced at all over a 30-year span or even longer. Keep in mind, though, that it is the engineering view on life that is relevant: how long a piece of equipment is assumed to be used. The accountant's view on life expectancy has no place here. Engineering might say 30 years; the accountant, 10.

# STRUCTURE AND INFRASTRUCTURE CAPEXES

Beyond those four questions, there is another category of capex needs that are part of the BA: the capex needs of the structures and sites' infrastructure. While not directly part of the production equipment, per se, repairs and replacements of the structures— for example, buildings, warehouses, and roofs—as well as infrastructure—such as railway spurs, utility systems, fencing, pipelines, channel dredging, and road repairs—still require capex outlays and, therefore, affect the company's operating cash flow.

Regarding structures, in many cases, relevant replacement values for most buildings have already been determined by the business's insurance company. The buildings and their insurance valuations can be included as part of the asset mapping as one lump sum. We usually assume the buildings were built when the site was built and assume they will live "forever" unless there are issues with them that would make us question that assumption. We always ask if there are issues with the buildings. It is not unusual that $2 million every three years will be capitalized in building repairs. Will the roof need replacement? How much will that project cost, and when will it be necessary?

With respect to infrastructure, the team starts by listing specific, known replacement needs, such as fencing or a railway replacement. The need is quantified, and the necessary timing is assumed. Estimating replacement costs for the rest of the site would require the team to do quite a bit of legwork for the miles of utility pipes, fencing, electrical cabling, and more. Since we've designed our process to be as practical as possible, we've discovered that estimating 15% of the total replacement costs of all production assets at a site is a fairly accurate figure to approximate these infrastructure replacement values.*

We typically assume that this replacement value was acquired when the mill was first built, and that it will last.

# ASSET MAPPING OUTPUT

The asset mapping work will result in two outputs. First, it will create a long-term capex plan that will go into the base alternative's cash flow for each facility.

Second, it will create a strategic asset ledger, based on replacement costs and not historic acquisition costs for all assets in use at the facility. A total replacement cost is calculated for the facility that should typically be 30% higher than it would cost to build a greenfield with the same capacity. It is more expensive to replace a facility in bits and pieces (which is what happens in the base alternative) than a complete greenfield project.

Figure 7.1 is an example of an asset mapping output, using a common illustration.

---

* This is a simplification to say the least; specific numbers can be applied per industry, of course.

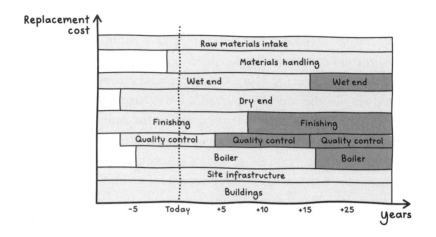

In this simplified case, the facility consists of nine assets, all of which are over the replacement cost threshold; this company has chosen $1 million as its threshold. Some were built/acquired several years before the analysis since the facility has been in operation for decades. Half of the assets, including buildings and site infrastructure, will not be replaced during the next 20 years. Assets such as the wet end, finishing, quality control systems, and boiler will need to be replaced if the facility is to sustain itself from an equipment point of view and keep its customers happy. The quality control systems have a short standard life and need replacement every 8 to 10 years. Management realizes that there is a larger accumulated capex need around 15 years out of the wet end, quality control systems, and the boiler. The mill's EBITDA must at that point be sufficient to even start considering the first two (the quality control system and the wet end) given their substantial costs.

# ADDITIONAL SMALL-SCALE CAPEXES

The asset mapping for the BA will identify the assumed capex needs. The team creates a comprehensive list of "major" capexes (those over the threshold) that will be required over the time period of the economic model. Those are identified, named, quantified, and roughly scheduled. As mentioned in Chapter 6, the BA must also take into account estimated capexes for environmental regulations and safety standards.

In addition to all of that, the team must also consider the inevitable "small-scale" capexes that will crop up over the years. A few comparatively smaller capexes at one site can easily and quickly add up to the equivalent of a major capex. To account for these, and to cover unexpected capexes, we've found that calculating a percentage of the total site's replacement cost today suffices. The basic rationale is that the more assets in use at a site, the higher the need for related small-scale capexes. Our clients' teams typically estimate these unspecified capexes costs between 0.3% and 0.5% each year of the total cost to replace the entire site. However, in different industries, we have seen teams use as little as 0.1% or as high as 0.8%. Practically speaking, these small-scale capexes will not have a material impact on which strategic alternative is chosen, but they should be accounted for in the BA nevertheless.

## The Strategic Asset Ledger

The result of the team's asset mapping is what we call a "strategic asset ledger." The ledger is catogorized by site and include:

- All known and necessary capexes required to maintain the site's ability to deliver to customers long term
- Structure and infrastructure capexes, including specific, known needs as well as a percentage of the total cost of replacing all the site's production assets
- Small-scale production capexes, calculated as a percentage of the site's total replacement cost

# THE BASE
# ALTERNATIVE:
# CASH FLOWS

While the engineers and site experts do the asset mapping exercise described in the previous chapter, the controllers gather the EBITDA split data according to a certain structure. This structure is different from industry to industry and needs to be set up to enable future simulations. These cash flows are not only per site; they are also per each site's major production asset where applicable. There are two categories:

1. Production volumes, pricing, and variable costs
2. FTEs/headcount and remaining fixed costs such as maintenance and overhead/selling, general, and administrative (SG&A)

# VARIABLE CASH FLOWS

For each site, what have the historic volumes, price, and variable cost developments been?* The team should gather this data from the previous five years' worth of records, typically. For the purposes of Superior Paper, we explain it here as being from one baseline year, but in reality the team should look back over the past five years.

The next step is to assign these values as closely as possible to a major asset, such as a production line or an individual machine. What has the volume produced per line been? What has the market price per output unit been (be that measured in tons, square feet/meters, liters, or whatever the case may be)? Then the team must also assign the variable costs of inputs. These include the price per unit of raw materials, energy consumption costs, and transportation costs.

For simplicity's sake, we're going to assume Superior Paper's mills have only one production line per mill.† Going through the exercise of recording production volumes and costs, the team might summarize its findings per site as shown in Table 8.1.

Table 8.1

| London | Base Year |
|---|---|
| Capacity | 200 |
| Production | 195 |
| Price/Unit | $0.50 |
| Variable Direct Costs/Unit | −$0.20 |
| Freight Costs/Unit | −$0.10 |

---

* It actually starts with understanding the "flowcharts" of the sites. Raw material flows, waste and by-product flows, energy flows, end product flows, and so on.

† The full cash flow model as used would potentially include 300 to 400 line items for an integrated steel or paper mill, accounting for input volumes, energy flows, and so on. For a small facility, such as a converting plant, it may be only 25 line items.

That is, the London mill has a capacity of 200 units and, on average for the past five years, has produced 195 units every year. The market price over the past five years has averaged $0.50 per unit. It costs London $0.20 per unit to manufacture and an additional $0.10 per unit to transport it to their customers.

# FTES/HEADCOUNT, OVERHEAD/SG&A, AND MAINTENANCE

The team must also account for the labor costs at each site as well as maintenance, other fixed costs, and overhead costs. The economic model usually treats these two categories as fixed (or, at least, quasi-fixed) costs. Labor costs are usually measured in full-time equivalent employees (FTEs) and can be split into operators, maintenance, and so on. Then the cost per FTE is added. Maintenance costs (contractors, materials) are included as well as other fixed costs (security, property tax, etc.). Overhead/SG&A includes, for instance, the costs of administration, sales, and so forth. These costs are important to get right when later considering expansions or consolidations (Will more people need to be hired?) or closures (What are the cost savings of avoiding a site's upkeep?).

# BASE YEAR CASH FLOWS

With each site's cash flows mapped, the team now has a site-specific cash flow model with data for the base year—not from an accounting perspective but a production perspective. Specifically, each site's EBITDA cash flows. In most industries, this is a practical approach to cash flow (before other cash flow items such as taxes, change in working capital, and capital expenditures that are added in the next step; we only account for those in projected future years).

Once Superior Paper's team maps London's EBITDA for the base year, it has Table 8.2.

Table 8.2

| London | Base Year |
|---|---|
| Capacity | 200 |
| Production | 195 |
| Price/unit | $0.54 |
| Variable Direct Costs/Unit | −$0.20 |
| Freight Costs/Unit | −$0.10 |

| Sales | $105 |
|---|---|
| Variable Direct Costs | −$39 |
| Freight Costs | −$19 |
| Fixed Costs | −$20 |
| EBITDA | $27 |
| EBITDA Margin | 26% |

From sales of $105, London contributes $27 in annual EBITDA.

After the team does the same for its other three sites, it finally has a comprehensive, systemwide economic baseline. Now is the time to check with reported EBITDA for the past years to make sure everything is captured. (See Table 8.3.)

Table 8.3

| System | Base Year |
|---|---|
| Total Demand | 855 units |
| Total Capacity | 945 units |
| Total Production | 855 units |
| Sales | $427 |
| EBITDA Margin | 20% |
| $CO_2$ Emissions | 454 ktons |

Although Superior Paper has a production capacity of 945 units across its four mills, the European market's demand on their products is only 855 units, leaving almost 100 units of excess capacity.

# PROJECTED CASH FLOWS

The team now has the system's EBITDA for the base year. Next, they need to project the line items in the EBITDA into the future. In our example, Superior Paper has decided on a time period of 20 years.

The uncertainty and even the failures around capital expenditure projects rarely come from a lack of data. In fast-moving markets, a model forecasting one year may be looking too far into the future. But due to the nature of capital-intensive industries, things happen far more gradually. Five-, 10-, or even 25-year forecasts can be reliable when applying some logic to the relationships between input variables.

Our clients always have either forecasting experts on their team or access to such. These subject matter experts can make relevant assumptions on future price changes and trends, freight costs, material costs and availability, how product quality demand and overall market demand will change, and more, with quality sufficient to establish the baseline. Everyone knows that all predictions about the future regarding pricing will be wrong, but that is OK—we are not trying to predict prices here, we are trying to establish the best possible capex strategy. It is a game predicting data that most companies are basically as good or bad at as the next one. The final conclusions will usually not rely on individual data being right or wrong.

Knowing that the forecasts will be wrong is one thing, but we claim that there are some fundamental laws that govern price and cost escalations long term and that any company does itself a big disservice by ignoring them.

## The Danger of Seeing Only Your Own Industry

Ole Terland, senior vice president of strategy for the Swedish forestry company SCA, pointed out:

> You can't just look at your industry when planning future trends. You have to look outside your industry to get the full picture. In the paper industry, we have seen a demand increase in our industry for years now. This cannot continue; things don't grow to heaven. It's easy to assume that our demand will continue to rise because recent history makes it seem like it will. But in our industry, you're investing for 20 or 30 years out. You have to have the broader view of what's happening to your customer behavior and trends in adjacent segments over a long time. You also have to look at cost developments in other market segments. Otherwise, you'll focus too much on your own business and miss the greater trends. It puts blinders on you so that you only foresee one future outcome. Think about printing paper demand and not seeing the internet impact and attractiveness of social media for advertising. You need to see brand owners' marketing trends, digitalization opportunities, and of course the attractiveness of your own paper and the full cost of using paper for publishing news or advertising. Just look at how plastic packaging suppliers are missing the attractiveness of fiber-based easy recyclable and sustainable products!

Knowing that our forecasts will be wrong, we must make our models testable. We need to be able to challenge our models with questions such as: What happens if pricing is off by X percent? Future cash flow will go up or down accordingly, but will our conclusion of the best possible *capex strategy* change? It may be difficult to completely buy in at this stage, but we rarely find that reasonable sensitivity analyses change which capex strategy is most desirable in any great order of magnitude (the great exception being when total output significantly differs between strategic options).

This is why it's critical to the capex strategy model that the company's best and brightest are in the room. While these experts can't predict the future, their expertise allows them to make reasonable assumptions about the price and cost inflation over the coming years. They can provide guidance on how company sales are expected to perform, how freight costs might rise or fall, what the price of gas might be, the rate of productivity improvements available in the future, how product quality and overall market demand are likely to change, and so forth.

Everyone knows that estimates are just best guesses about the future. The purpose of the economic model isn't to predict prices—it's to allow the team to compare different capex strategies. As long as price and cost inflation are assumed to be the same, logically for all sites and all strategic alternatives (SAs), it doesn't affect the *relative* positions of the competing strategic alternatives to each other much. If pricing turns out to be 2% lower than expected, then *all* SAs' value curves will shift down—but the best SA's value curve on top is still likely to be on top; the worst SA's curve is still likely to be at the bottom.

Additionally, when the team begins running different SAs, it will perform sensitivity tests to ask such questions as, What if there are cost overruns? What if freight costs go higher than expected? That's the usefulness of a holistic method-based economic model—the team can explore endless possibilities by changing the parameters and/or variables inside the model on the go.

Focusing again on just the London mill, the team makes the projections in Table 8.4.

Table 8.4

| London | Base Year | Year 1 | Year 2 | Year 5 | Year 10 | Year 20 |
|---|---|---|---|---|---|---|
| Capacity | 200.0 | 200.0 | 200.0 | 200.0 | 200.0 | 200.0 |
| Production | 195.0 | 197.0 | 198.9 | 200.0 | 200.0 | 200.0 |
| Price/Unit | 0.54 | 0.55 | 0.55 | 0.57 | 0.60 | 0.66 |
| Variable Direct Costs/Unit | −0.20 | −0.20 | −0.21 | −0.22 | −0.23 | −0.27 |
| Freight Costs/Unit | −0.10 | −0.10 | −0.10 | −0.11 | −0.12 | −0.13 |
| | | | | | | |
| Sales | 105.3 | 107.4 | 109.6 | 113.5 | 119.3 | 131.8 |
| Variable Direct Costs | −39.0 | −40.0 | −41.0 | −43.1 | −46.4 | −53.9 |
| Freight Costs | −19.3 | −19.8 | −20.3 | −21.4 | −23.0 | −26.7 |
| Fixed Costs | −20.0 | −20.5 | −21.0 | −22.6 | −25.6 | −32.8 |
| EBITDA | 27.0 | 27.1 | 27.3 | 26.4 | 24.3 | 18.4 |
| EBITDA Margin | 26% | 25% | 25% | 23% | 20% | 14% |
| | | | | | | |
| Change in Working Capital | – | −1.0 | −1.0 | −1.1 | −1.1 | −1.2 |
| Tax | – | −5.4 | −5.5 | −5.3 | −4.9 | −3.7 |
| Capex | – | −5.0 | −3.0 | −11.0 | −4.0 | −4.0 |
| Cash Flow | – | 15.7 | 17.8 | 9.1 | 14.3 | 9.5 |
| $CO_2$ Emissions | 117 | 118 | 120 | 121 | 123 | 127 |

Because there are no strategic capexes in the base alternative (BA), London's capacity will remain the same. Demand is predicted to rise; by year three, London should be running right at peak capacity. Although the price per unit will rise, its production and freight costs will rise, too. As such, London's EBITDA margin will continually decline over the next 20 years (thanks to technology/scale improvements driving creative destruction). Note that the team is also tracking $CO_2$ emissions over time.

In the first year, London's EBITDA is projected to be $27. The EBITDA is merged with the result from the BA's asset mapping, which provides a systematically produced, long-term capex fore-cast. Then, changes in working capital are added as well as a corporate tax calculation on the EBITDA, considering tax depreciation from all the capexes (the output of the asset mapping). Capital expenditures are deducted, too. Net, the mill will contribute a net cash flow of $15.70 for Superior Paper.

Once the team projects these same cash flows for each site, the economic model returns the site-specific accumulated discounted cash flow curves in Figure 8.1.

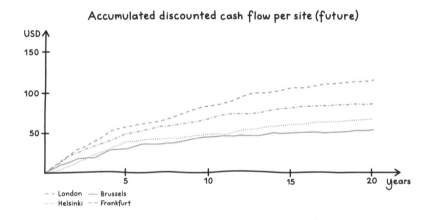

Previously, the team discovered London had the highest EBITDA margins. Here, the team sees that London also contributes the highest accumulated discounted cash flow to the system. From these two pieces of information, some on the team may start prioritizing London in their minds, unconsciously giving it preferential treatment. After all, the data shows that it's clearly superior to the other sites. Again, a site's performance in isolation tells the team *nothing* about how it interacts with the system. The team cannot and should not draw any conclusions until it begins running SAs.

Adding all four sites together results in the BA value curve for the entire company shown in Figure 8.2.

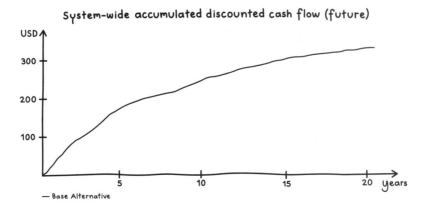

For the first time in the company's history, Superior Paper has a macro-level, realistic perspective, including its thoroughly mapped capex needs, of what the future could look like. Furthermore, this *is the best estimate* of what the future would look like absent any strategic intent.

Some believe the BA is a poor alternative. When we get to this point in a project and the base alternative often does not look very good, we sometimes hear, "We would never run our site like this; our company would do much better than the base alternative." That could be debated (but does not need to be because the work on what they should do as opposed to the baseline has not yet begun). However, these challengers are wrong: most companies do worse than their base alternative. What we demonstrated in the earlier chapters of this book is that when applying strategic intent, companies lower value. They do not put together a capex plan that creates value because they chase short paybacks, resulting in lower company cash flow. They end up with a curve lower than that of the base alternative, because they do not carefully design the company's strategy and capital allocation long term. Instead, they shoot from the hip, reacting to individual needs and opportunities, motivated by arguments and measures irrelevant to capital allocation. They continually do this every year; from a value creation point of view, never improving their company from where it is today.

## Capex Strategy Keystone

*Only use accumulated discounted cash flow curves to present and compare capex strategy cash flows.*

In phases I and II, Superior Paper created its economic model and projected the BA. In the next phase, the team will begin compiling a list of several potential strategic capex projects that it *could* pursue. It won't be until phase IV that Superior Paper can begin looking at which combinations of capex projects it *should* pursue.

# 9

# STRATEGIC BUILDING BLOCKS

At the end of the project team's first month of using its new capex approach, the company's leadership joins the team to review the base alternative together and the assumptions made. At the end of the meeting, being influenced by the outcome of the base alternative, the full team will ask itself a question: What are the larger, more strategic opportunities at each site?

It doesn't matter whether they're "good" or "bad" projects. Seen in isolation, they can't be accurately judged. It's only by stringing a number of these individual capex projects together, and by running the projections through the capex strategy model, that the team can see how these different projects together in different combinations affect overall long-term system cash flow.

By "strategic" capexes, we mean capital expenditures that change something vital in the company, that have the ability to move the needle. In our experience, such strategic investments include:

- Expansion of existing assets' capacities
- Addition of capabilities
- Conversion of sites
- Other major rebuilds of existing assets

- Line closures in a site
- Complete site closures
- Brownfields and greenfields
- Acquisition of other sites

Each production site should have somewhere between 5 and 10 such opportunities—what we call strategic building blocks, or SBBs. An SBB is only for one site. There is never one SBB that covers activities on two sites—that would require two separate SBBs. For Superior Paper with four mills, that would mean between 20 and 40 SBBs, plus a few more for potential greenfields and acquisitions. (For ease of explanation, Superior Paper's team will identify only 14.)

We think of these building blocks like Lego blocks. One of the writers of *The Lego Movie*, Christopher Miller, has been quoted as saying, "With a bucket of Legos, you can tell any story. You can build an airplane or a dragon or a pirate ship—it's whatever you can imagine." The same is true with SBBs: you can easily tell whatever business story you want. However, you have to create the building blocks in the first place.

The first SBB the team considers is addressing Helsinki's quality issue. While the Finnish site has a capacity of 240 units, it can only sell 180 units of its slightly inferior quality product. The team could fix the quality issue, thereby freeing up an additional 60 units of capacity. However, the company already has excess capacity. By itself, fixing the issue at Helsinki doesn't make much sense. The team creates the SBB anyway just in case it might be needed later. Team members estimate the capex amount and the possibly avoided capital that is in the base alternative (i.e., by spending more capital now, they avoid the future capex projects they would have otherwise needed to do). The team also estimates any changes to variable and fixed costs. The SBB now carries the data (compared to the base alternative) for this specific project.

Another option might be to close the aging mill altogether. But where would its 180 units of production go? Is it worth keeping that volume? When a team starts shifting production quantities from one site to various sites across the portfolio to the degree that is possible from a capability point of view, we call this the "carousel."* The carousel can be a manually operated Excel spreadsheet or a supply chain optimization tool providing a new production optimization based on the new production footprint.

When the team begins carouselling Helsinki's production elsewhere, it quickly runs up against a problem: even combined, the other three mills don't have the excess capacity to absorb 180 units of production. Again, the team goes ahead and creates the SBB for a closure of Helsinki, knowing that it will probably need to be combined with other, soon-to-be created SBBs that include an increase in capacity and possibly added capabilities somewhere else. The team can't start running alternative projections because it hasn't set up any of those types of SBBs yet; the SBB at hand focuses only on the changes to the system from closing Helsinki.

## The Cost of a Capex Project

Obviously for most SBBs, there is the required capex investment: the turnkey cost of the project. The complexity comes into play when you consider how that one change ripples throughout the production ecosystem. How does the decision affect new costs and how does it result in cost savings?

- Capital expenditures avoided
- Marginal increase of raw material costs
- Specific energy consumption changes
- Cost of shipping and storing extra raw material
- Cost of storing and shipping finished product
- Additional equipment to handle higher volumes downstream

---

* Thanks to Guillum Buisson-Street at Sappi for this word. He used it in an engagement to describe this type of modelling with volumes and we've used it ever since.

- The demand for water, electricity, and other utilities
- Waste by-product and cost of disposal
- Labor costs for running at higher production
- Change in selling, general, and administrative expenses
- Change in maintenance costs
- Environmental cleanup
- Severance/redundancy costs
- Leases/contracts broken
- Land or equipment sold

Overall, which data points to address per SBB will depend on the industry and the details of the full cash flow model.

The team continues working on the data for the closure of Helsinki SBB. There is a need to consider closure costs, such as the required environmental outlays from shutting down a production site, plus severance for employees, and so on. Will contracts be breached? On the other hand, the SBB avoids all the necessary capexes Helsinki would otherwise require (as accounted for in the baseline). Maybe there is the revenue from the sale of the site's land. Then, too, there are the future labor and overhead costs avoided. After calculating the figures, the results of this SBB look like Table 9.1.

**Table 9.1**

| Helsinki | Capex | Avoided Capex | Environmental and Other Closure Costs | Redundancy Costs | Sale of Land and Equipment | Capacity Effect | Fixed Cost Effect | Variable Cost Effect | Working Capital Effect |
|---|---|---|---|---|---|---|---|---|---|
| Close | 0 | 100% | −25 | −30 | 5 | −240 | −100% | −100% | 10 |

Even though all SBBs are supposed to be created before running any strategic alternatives, the team wants to better understand how the economic model works. So, the team creates a strategic alternative with just this one closure SBB and names it SA1. Table 9.2 shows what they found.

Table 9.2

| | Capacity | Volume Produced | Price/Unit | Freight Costs/ Unit | $CO_2$/Unit Produced |
|---|---|---|---|---|---|
| Base Alternative | 945 | 864 | 0.50 | −0.11 | 0.53 |
| SA1 | 710 | 710 | 0.50 | −0.11 | 0.53 |

As expected, total capacity dropped by Helsinki's 240 units or so. The remaining three mills would operate at full capacity. Superior Paper would still produce the same amount of carbon emissions per unit. Freight costs per unit would remain unchanged, too. (With each SBB, the supply chain optimization team steps in to determine how best to spread production across the four mills.) But more importantly, the team wants to know how Helsinki's closure affects the company's overall cash flow. In Figure 9.1, the capex strategy model graphs the base alternative as well as SA1.

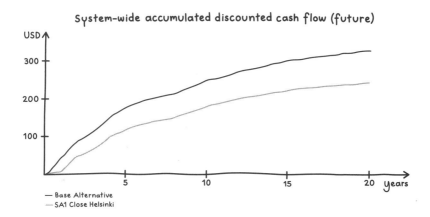

System-wide accumulated discounted cash flow (future)

— Base Alternative
···· SA1 Close Helsinki

As the team intuitively knew, closing Helsinki and doing nothing else would negatively impact cash flow. With this graph, however, the team can see the magnitude that closure would have. By itself, this would be a bad strategic move. That does not, however, mean it's a bad SBB. The work has just begun.

## The Human Element

As Annica Bresky, CEO of Stora Enso, says in the Afterword, the decision to close a site isn't an easy one.

Fortunately for those involved in industrial sites, a closure typically takes quite some time, allowing the company to relocate, retrain, or otherwise ethically transition employees elsewhere. We've observed that the stronger the social safety net—and we hold Sweden up as a potential example—the easier it is for companies to make capitalist decisions like these (favoring companies' competitiveness and the nation's growth and attractiveness) Cultural factors could move things in the other direction with France being perceived as one such example.

The team then considers another SBB: What if instead of closing Helsinki, its capacity is expanded and its quality issue addressed? But there is a choice as the team has identified two different ways to solve for existing bottlenecks: one would increase capacity by 30 units; the other, by 50. The team makes an SBB for each option. Who knows what this can possibly be combined with?

The team decides to create similar debottlenecking SBBs for Brussels and Frankfurt while finding that London doesn't have such an option. If the team were to summarize each of those strategic capex projects as a playing card, the potential playing deck would look like Figure 9.2.

## Debottleneck
## Helsinki +30

- −$20 capex
- +$4 avoided capex
- +30 tons capacity
- −$1.50 fixed costs
- +2% var. costs
- −$2 wrkg capital

## Debottleneck
## Helsinki +50

- −$32 capex
- +$6 avoided capex
- +50 tons capacity
- −$1.70 fixed costs
- +2% var. costs
- −$3 wrkg capital

## Debottleneck
## Brussels +25

- −$30 capex
- +$4 avoided capex
- +25 tons capacity
- −$2 fixed costs
- +0% var. costs
- −$1.50 wrkg capital

## Debottleneck
## Frankfurt +70

- −$68 capex
- +$1 avoided capex
- +70 tons capacity
- −$2 fixed costs
- +0% var. costs
- −$5 wrkg capital

## Debottleneck
## Frankfurt +100

- −$75 capex
- +$2 avoided capex
- +100 tons capacity
- −$3 fixed costs
- +0% var. costs
- −$5 wrkg capital

By this point, the team is curious. Running the economic model without Helsinki makes the team wonder what the individual effects of closure SBBs would be for the other three mills. However, that would be jumping ahead in the process. First, the SBBs for all alternatives must be created.

> *A "rule" we have when doing a capex strategy project for a client is that we create a closure SBB for each site. That includes the best sites, the "favorite child," and the site where the CEO began his or her career. Doing so releases a lot of tension in the team, as this activity means that we are not singling out any site. As a result, the project team is eager to look at all other SBBs and combinations of SBBs after this type of exercise. When creating the SBBs, we do not know if it is maybe the favorite site that needs to close. In fact, we don't know if any sites should be closed; it's too soon to tell. We are simply creating as many cards as we can so we can make as many "plays" as possible.*

In addition to increasing capacity on existing production lines, the team also considers building a brownfield at London. Besides all of this, leadership revealed in the initial kickoff meeting that it has been considering acquiring a paper mill in Madrid. This results in two more SBBs: one of simply acquiring the mill and the other for acquiring the mill and immediately closing it (effectively buying its market demand). Leadership expects to pay $53 for Madrid, based on a conservative EBITDA multiple of six. After visiting the Spanish site, the asset mapping team has estimated $60 in capex needs over the next 10 years.

At the end of the two days, the project team has a list of 14 total SBBs:

### London
- Close
- Debottleneck +15 units
- Convert
- Brownfield

### Helsinki
- Close
- Debottleneck +30 units + quality upgrade
- Debottleneck +50 units + quality upgrade

### Brussels
- Close
- Debottleneck +25 units

### Frankfurt
- Close
- Debottleneck +70 units
- Debottleneck +100 units

### Madrid
- Acquire
- Acquire and close

With its full "playing deck," the project team is ready to play for keeps.

## Don't Discuss Dynamic Pricing

*We caution our clients that they absolutely cannot assume any dynamic upward price effects on their products as an effect of capacity closures. Price changes may be a natural consequence of an effective capex strategy, but assuming them can easily be misconstrued as a price-fixing scheme and/or monopolistic practice. A capex strategy needs to be motivated by other effects than dynamic price assumptions.*

# 10

# STRATEGIC
# ALTERNATIVES

With 14 strategic building blocks (SBBs) now created, the team has already seen the effect that closing Helsinki would have on the system. The decision is made to continue by analyzing what each mill contributes to the system on its own, starting with London. The team runs the economic model using the single SBB closure playing card, labeling this run as SA2 (strategic alternative 2) and Figure 10.1 is the result.

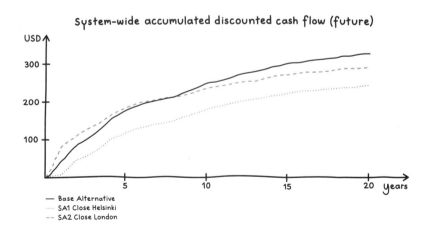

Well, now *this* is quite surprising. Despite London having the highest EBITDA margins and contributing the most cash flow to the system, the model shows that Superior Paper wouldn't lose nearly as much cash flow (compared to the base alternative [BA]) if they closed London, than it would closing Helsinki. Part of this is because the real estate under the London mill is worth a fortune; a net cash value to the company of $100. By closing London, the company would actually increase accumulated cash flows for the first seven years *even if it did nothing else.* That, in itself, is revelatory to Superior Paper.

Next, the team does the same SAs for Brussels and Frankfurt, and Figure 10.2 is the result.

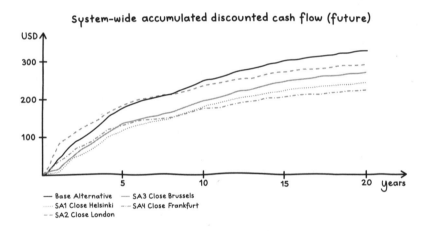

While none of these strategic alternatives are viable options (they all decrease the BA's cash flow in the long term), the curves are quite telling. The biggest gap is between the BA and a Frankfurt closure. That means Frankfurt is the biggest contributor to Superior Paper's cash flow system—the one that brings the most value. The smallest gap is between the BA and London's closure. That means London contributes the least to Superior Paper when the production portfolio is viewed as an interconnected cash flow system. None of this means the team should recommend a closure, but it does give some clues as to where some of the capex opportunities might be hiding.

## A Diamond in the Rough

For capital allocation purposes, you cannot determine the value of the production asset by valuing or discounting a site's future cash flow. You cannot determine it by looking at its EBITDA margin, much less its ROCE, EVA, or other such measures. You can only understand the performance and value of a site by comparing two different alternatives to each other:

1. The accumulated discounted cash flow of the whole system with the production asset
2. The accumulated discounted cash flow of the whole system without the production asset

One pressing issue is whether Superior Paper should pursue the Madrid acquisition. After running the "acquire Madrid" playing card, the capex strategy model shows that the acquisition would never be recovered in terms of accumulated discounted cash flow. This is typical of what we see in a majority of studied acquisition cases. It should be noted, however, that we work with several clients who have become extremely astute in selecting the right targets and have used this skill to improve overall systemwide accumulated discounted cash flow. Correctly used, acquisitions can be powerful vehicles for value creation—*if* leadership has the right analysis and the mindset of acting on the implied consequences of acquisitions without hesitation. But for Superior Paper, Madrid should be a nonstarter.

With the acquisition question put to rest, the team turns its attention back to maximizing cash flow within the company's existing portfolio of sites. SA2—closing the London line—seems intriguing, so the team decides to play different SBB cards to see the effects. The line of thinking is that if the London mill contributes the least to the system from a value point of view, perhaps it would make sense to close it and carousel its production with an increased capacity somewhere else.

The third, fourth, and fifth SAs were devoted to looking at each site's value contribution. In the sixth SA, the team plays the SBB card of closing London combined with the card of upgrading and debottlenecking Helsinki to increase capacity by 30 units. Although the model returns with a value curve still lower than the BA, it's better than SA2's curve. While the team still hasn't found a viable option to the base alternative, it seems like there's some promise in pursuing this line of thinking.

Iterating further with SA7, the team plays the same "close London" card but pairs it with the "debottleneck Frankfurt +70" card. This time, the difference between the two curves (the BA and SA7) is almost negligible. So even though SA7 still isn't superior to the BA, things are headed in the right direction.

The team has tried increasing capacity by 30 units then by 70 units. What if there was one expansion in Frankfurt of 100 units? In SA8, the team runs the model of closing London while simultaneously debottlenecking Frankfurt by 100 units. The model returns Figure 10.3.

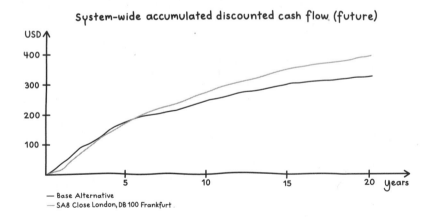

System-wide accumulated discounted cash flow (future)

— Base Alternative
— SA8 Close London, DB 100 Frankfurt

Success! The team has the first strategic alternative that generates at least 20% higher cash flow than the BA in the long term: $329 versus $397 in accumulated discounted cash flows over 20 years. There's a slight dip initially to account for the capex outlays of expanding Frankfurt, but by year six, SA8's accumulated discounted cash flow begins outpacing the BA's. While any company would welcome a strategy that promised an increase in accumulated discounted cash flow, the goal of our process is to maximize cash flow. The team can't know if other strategic combinations would turn out to be even better until all are tried.

Staying with the London closure as a cornerstone of current iterations, the team looks at debottlenecking Frankfurt by only 70 units but addressing the quality problem and debottlenecking Helsinki to increase capacity there by 50 units. The model returns the numbers in Table 10.1 for the ninth SA.

**Table 10.1**

| | Capacity | Volume Produced | Price/Unit | Freight Costs/Unit | $CO_2$/Unit Produced |
|---|---|---|---|---|---|
| Base Alternative | 945 | 864 | 0.50 | −0.11 | 0.53 |
| SA9 | 870 | 860 | 0.50 | −0.12 | 0.46 |

Since 100 units is only half of London's capacity, it's not surprising that overall capacity fell. But after the other three mills absorbed its production, along with two expansions, Superior Paper would still have enough capacity to just meet all of its market demand. The team is excited about the 13% drop in $CO_2$ emissions per unit produced. The freight costs of shipping to London's customers would raise the average rate of transportation. The bigger question, of course, is how all of these affect the company's cash flow, which is shown in Figure 10.4.

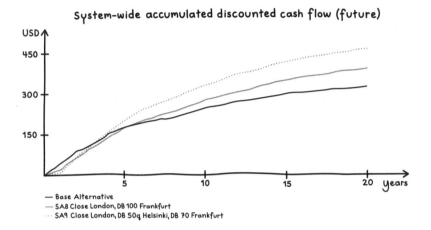

System-wide accumulated discounted cash flow (future)

— Base Alternative
— SA8 Close London, DB 100 Frankfurt
··· SA9 Close London, DB 50q Helsinki, DB 70 Frankfurt

> There's always a bit of an aha moment when you see the different scenarios graphed against each other.
>
> **—Toby Lawton, CFO, SCA**

The accumulated discounted cash flow increased by an astonishing 43% over the BA. Plus, SA9 only takes three years before it's on par with the BA. The gap rapidly increases after that. The team decides that iteration went well but would like to mix and match other combinations. The team experiments with closing Brussels and expanding London, then closing Brussels and expanding Helsinki, and so forth. After a dozen or so iterations, no iteration beats SA9. The team decides to return to it and see if it can be marginally improved. In iteration 23, the team keeps the "close London" and "debottleneck Helsinki +50" cards on the table but upgrades the Frankfurt expansion to 100 units. In just a few seconds, changing the variable in the model gets the results in Figure 10.5.

While not as dramatic of an increase (only $20), it's still the highest one yet.

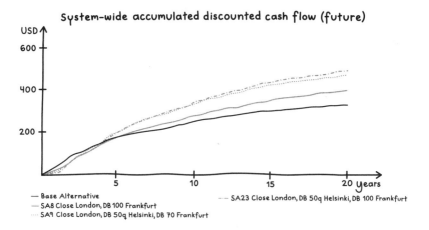

In a previous iterations, the team ran an SA that closed both London and Brussels, since these are the two most expensive sites to operate. While it didn't return as high of a cash flow as SA9, it did prompt one person on the team to ask, What if we created another SBB where we don't close Brussels but don't make any major capexes, either, for 10 years or so? That is, what if we just ran it for cash? After creating that individual SBB, the team returns to the economic model and runs four cards: close London, debottleneck Helsinki +70, debottleneck Frankfurt +100, and run Brussels for cash. SA24 comes back with the curve in Figure 10.6.

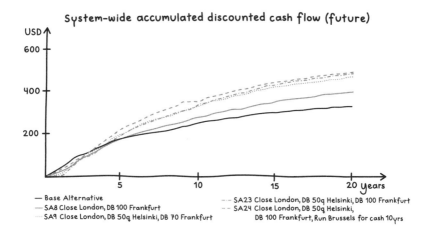

Success! The new SBB increased overall accumulated, discounted cash flows by an additional $5. The higher cash flow is especially prominent over the first 10 years, at which Superior Paper will still have some options with Brussels: closing, selling the mill off, or reinvesting in it.

The team tries a handful more SAs, but SA24 continues to be the best strategy. The final tally stands at Table 10.2.

Table 10.2

| | Capacity | Volume Produced | Price/Unit | Freight Costs/Unit | $CO_2$/Unit Produced |
|---|---|---|---|---|---|
| Base Alternative | 945 | 864 | 0.50 | −0.11 | 0.53 |
| SA24 | 900 | 869 | 0.50 | −0.12 | 0.45 |

Production volumes will go up by five units, thanks to some new capabilities. Though overall capacity is reduced, there's still ample room for growth, if need be. $CO_2$ emissions are reduced by 15%, an impressive amount. The average cost of shipping a ton of paper across the system will marginally rise, but an enviable 50% increase in cash flow should more than compensate for a 10% freight cost increase per unit.

The team summarizes its work in an "action matrix" shown in Table 10.3.

**Table 10.3**

| Region | Item | BA | SA1 | SA2 | SA3 | SA4 | SA5 | SA6 | SA7 | SA8 | SA9 | SA23 | SA24 |
|---|---|---|---|---|---|---|---|---|---|---|---|---|---|
| London | BA | × | × |  | × | × | × | ⋮ | ⋮ |  |  |  |  |
| London | Close |  |  | × |  |  |  | ⋮ | ⋮ | × | × | × | × |
| London | Debottleneck +15 |  |  |  |  |  |  | ⋮ | ⋮ |  |  |  |  |
| London | Covert |  |  |  |  |  |  | ⋮ | ⋮ |  |  |  |  |
| London | Brownfield |  |  |  |  |  |  | ⋮ | ⋮ |  |  |  |  |
| Helsinki | BA | × | × |  | × | × | × | ⋮ | ⋮ |  | × |  |  |
| Helsinki | Close |  |  | × |  |  |  | ⋮ | ⋮ |  |  |  |  |
| Helsinki | Debottleneck + 30 + quality upgrade |  |  |  |  |  |  | ⋮ | ⋮ |  |  |  |  |
| Helsinki | Debottleneck + 50 + quality upgrade |  |  |  |  |  |  | ⋮ | ⋮ |  | × | × | × |
| Brussels | BA | × | × | × |  | × | × | ⋮ | ⋮ | × | × | × |  |
| Brussels | Close |  |  |  |  | × |  | ⋮ | ⋮ |  |  |  |  |
| Brussels | Debottleneck + 25 |  |  |  |  |  |  | ⋮ | ⋮ |  |  |  |  |
| Brussels | Run for cash for 10 yrs. |  |  |  |  |  |  | ⋮ | ⋮ |  |  |  | × |
| Frankfurt | BA | × | × | × | × |  | × | ⋮ | ⋮ |  |  |  |  |
| Frankfurt | Close |  |  |  |  | × |  | ⋮ | ⋮ |  |  |  |  |
| Frankfurt | Debottleneck +70 |  |  |  |  |  |  | ⋮ | ⋮ |  |  | × |  |
| Frankfurt | Debottleneck +100 |  |  |  |  |  |  | ⋮ | ⋮ | × |  | × | × |
| Madrid | N/A | × | × | × | × | × |  | ⋮ | ⋮ | × | × | × | × |
| Madrid | Acquire |  |  |  |  |  | × | ⋮ | ⋮ |  |  |  |  |
| Total | Capacity | 945 | 710 | 750 | 740 | 645 | 1,145 | ⋮ | ⋮ | 850 | 870 | 900 | 900 |
| Total | Volume produced | 864 | 710 | 700 | 690 | 595 | 1,064 | ⋮ | ⋮ | 769 | 869 | 869 | 869 |
| Total | Price/unit | 0.50 | 0.50 | 0.49 | 0.50 | 0.51 | 0.50 | ⋮ | ⋮ | 0.50 | 0.50 | 0.50 | 0.50 |
| Total | $CO_2$/unit produced | 0.53 | 0.53 | 0.51 | 0.52 | 0.57 | 0.55 | ⋮ | ⋮ | 0.47 | 0.46 | 0.45 | 0.45 |
| Total | Freight cost/unit produced | -0.11 | -0.11 | -0.11 | -0.11 | -0.10 | -0.10 | ⋮ | ⋮ | -0.12 | -0.12 | -0.12 | -0.12 |

Of course, the chosen SA looks good as it stands currently, but what if some of the team's assumptions like price and market demand are wrong? In the next chapter, the team subjects the SA to a series of rigorous "stress tests" as it runs different macroeconomic scenarios to see whether SA24 remains valid.

The competitor to be feared is one who never bothers about you at all, but goes on making his own business better all the time.

—Henry Ford

## The True Cost of Mergers and Acquisitions

John Williams, CEO of Domtar Corporation (and author of our Foreword), puts it like this: "Statistics say that 70% of the time you acquire an asset, you've overpaid for it. After an acquisition, the asset's performance starts declining. The people tell you, 'We're underinvested.' So, off you go, trying to put in another billion dollars or two in the hopes it will solve the performance problem you've just purchased for a billion dollars. This happens every single day in the industry."

Superior Paper estimated the Madrid mill would require $60 in capital expenditures to maintain operations over the next 10 years. In our 25 years of being in trenches side-by-side with our clients' teams, we find that the vast majority of the time teams underestimate the total capex costs required.

Worse still, some companies don't even attempt to account for future capex needs. They go solely on the site's EBITDA multiples—another one of those irrelevant measures. Too many times, we have seen firsthand the dire results from this line of thinking. EBITDA multiples don't take into account capex needs at all. This is like buying a car for its market price and completely ignoring the fact it needs a new engine. If that weren't cause for concern enough, EBITDA multiples tend to overvalue older assets and undervalue newer ones; since it's usually older mills for sale, you can imagine the result.

Most of all, leadership views a potential M&A through an analytical lens, asking the black-or-white question: Is this a good buy? As our method demonstrates, it is impossible to gauge whether a strategic decision is good or bad in isolation. It's only through a systems-thinking lens that an individual site's true contribution to the portfolio can be discovered. The question is: How good can our company's accumulated discounted cash flow possibly be without the acquisition versus how good can our company's accumulated discounted cash flow possibly be with the acquisition? The answer to that question will not be the discounted cash flow from the acquisition target. The exception would be whether the acquisition target is a completely separate business from what you have today—but why would you buy such a business?

In our hypothetical case here, there's no question: acquiring Madrid isn't a feasible alternative if value creation is the goal.

The average success of acquisitions can be debated, and different companies have very different track records of succeeding in their acquisition strategies. There is abundant literature on rationales for acquisitions and the potential risks from an intention point of view. There are, however, a few common pitfalls that are rarely debated or understood at all.

Underestimating future capex needs comes from underestimating the replacement costs of new assets by focusing too much on the last few years of capex levels, depreciation, and book value. The last few years' capex levels rarely give any real indication of the true capex needs going forward to keep assets running. The sellers often "put lipstick on the pig" by underinvesting. Also, depreciation levels give little or no information regarding future investment needs. In fact, the correlation may even be negative. Low depreciation levels often indicate aging assets and large near-term reinvestment and/or consolidation needs. Then there are buyers who sometimes believe that the capital expenditures required do not matter since the capexes that will be made will have a positive NPV. Since the capex will "carry itself," these buyers don't believe they need to include those in acquisition analysis at all. This is a terribly costly misunderstanding.

Since the EBITDA in no way reflects future capex needs and the remaining life of the site's assets, it provides no linear information regarding enterprise value. Using standard industry multiples, even allowing for the accepted spread between attractive and unattractive targets, tends to undervalue new assets and perhaps more dangerously significantly overvalue aging ones—and again, the aging ones are typically the ones for sale.

As described in Chapter 6, all capital-intensive industries should assume continuously deteriorating terms of trade; in other words, the cost of the input goods will have higher cost escalations compared to the finished goods sold. That deterioration must continually be combatted by process, quality, and feature improvements. This means that a significant part of the capex amounts assumed to improve the business actually is used only to defend its current ability to generate cash flow.

Generally, acquisitions accelerate the optimal rate of consolidation of production capacity. In the extreme, a company with only one machine does not need to be able to take the amount of hard decisions regarding closures and technology change compared to a company that runs 10 sites with interchangeability. So, at least from a capex strategy point of view, larger companies need to be nimbler and faster compared to their smaller competitors when optimizing the value of capex allocation.

# SENSITIVITIES
# AND LIMITATIONS

Throughout the entire process, the team should ask: Do these numbers make sense? Do these figures add up? Do the data and calculations pass the gut test? Drawing on the depth and breadth of experience around the conference table, there should be a consensus that the economic model's assumptions and projections are realistic.

The team can and should do sensitivity tests for relevant strategic building blocks (SBBs). With Superior Paper, for instance, running Brussels for cash for the next 10 years incrementally bumped up the cash flow curve, but what if there were slightly more urgent capex needs than the team planned for? Or what if the closure costs of the London mill were greater than expected? Would the rest of the strategic alternatives (SAs) based on its closure still be viable options? When consolidating London, the team was especially aware of how transportation costs might vary, and it investigated how much extra cost the recommendation could tolerate. What if Frankfurt's expansion capex was understated? Or the startup curve to achieve expected volumes became longer? Perhaps where it only realized 90% of its promised output?

But these are capex-specific sensitivities. Once the team has settled on an SA—the one being considered as the recommendation for action (RfA)—these potential strategies needed to be subjected to systemic sensitivities, such as:

- **Price changes:** What would happen if prices fell faster than expected? Does the final RfA rest on an assumed capacity increase? Does it allow for a decrease in production volumes, if needed?

- **Market demand:** What if there's another global industry disruption like the financial crisis of 2008 and ensuing great recession or the Covid-19 pandemic? What if demand spikes or plummets? A good RfA should remain a viable option even under extreme demand changes. It is our experience that unexpected disruptions rarely change the recommendation for action, however, they do alter the optimal speed of executing the RfA, resulting in an acceleration of some decisions and allowing others to happen later. For instance, when the 2008 financial crisis occurred, we had some clients who knew how to respond to not only be resilient but to capitalize on the challenge. You must be so well acquainted with your options that you are never caught unprepared.

- **Capex needs:** What if the capex projects' costs needed to fulfill the recommendation significantly change? What if overall capex costs inflate faster than assumed?

- **Raw material, energy, labor, and capital costs:** What if they rise higher and/or more quickly than anticipated? Does the RfA still hold true? Or the opposite: What if cost inflation is lower than expected and/or the ability to recover it through pricing is higher than assumed?

- **Regulatory requirements:** What if Brazil tightens environmental regulations? What if the European Union mandates that manufacturers source a minimum level of energy from renewable resources?

- **Currency fluctuations:** What if the pound sterling suddenly weakened against the euro? Would it still make sense to sell London? These questions are even more important in local economies where exchange rates are more volatile.
- **Environmental sustainability:** Has the company committed to curbing its $CO_2$ emissions by a certain date? Has it committed to sourcing a certain amount of raw material from sustainable sources?

After submitting the candidates for the RfA to these types of sensitivity tests, the Superior Paper team found that few sensitivities changed the relative attractiveness between alternatives in a significant way. The valuations changed a lot, but not the ranking of alternatives since all the alternatives moved up or down in virtual lockstep. In the few cases where the preferred alternative did lose its number one rank, it remained a solid number two or three, just behind various alternatives that analytically benefited from the specific sensitivity. So, the preferred alternative never went bad; no other alternatives came close to being as robust and the team felt confident that even in unexpected scenarios, its best SAs remain valid. The team made sure to understand what options existed if the unexpected happened. The only remaining unknown and explored going forward was what to do in Brussels and when. While running it for cash, the team built plans for an early exit and for using the site as a brownfield or expansion.

## What If . . . ?

Of course, executives want to know, What if . . . ? For instance, what if the market price for a company's product goes up or down by 5%? Would the chosen alternative still be the best way to go?

If we were to graph both cash flows for each of those scenarios (a price increase of 5% as well as the same decrease) for a company's base alternative (BA) and a given SA, we would arrive at Figure 11.1.

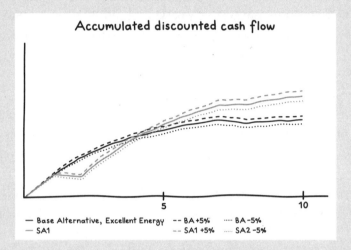

The absolute numbers of one alternative over another do not matter. It's their position in relation to each other. If prices fall by 5%, SA1 is still the superior choice here because in this scenario we can assume that it will happen in the BA, too. If prices rise by the same amount, we see the same story. Therefore, even if the underlying assumptions of the analysis are wrong (and, to some degree, they inevitably will be), the curves still clearly depict the winner of the two.

Traditional capex delta calculations, done on a project-by-project basis, are quite sensitive to changes like this. If an underlying assumption changes just slightly, these measures may indicate the capex project isn't viable at all. This happens when you look at only the delta, and not what happens on a company level. Enterprisewide analyses are not at all that sensitive; whatever you test in a sensitivity will happen to all the alternatives, so all these curves will move up or down. Here the question is: Do the rankings change?

These types of holistic analyses give company leaders the confidence to move forward with a resilient capex strategy, confident that it's the right call while simultaneously knowing its assumptions won't be perfect.

We have seen situations where the leadership of a company procrastinates due to assumption's uncertainty. These leaders might procrastinate for one to three years, which is very costly since they have postponed traveling on the path they should be down. The losses from procrastinating quickly become more expensive than the cost of uncertainty.

## Consistency of Assumptions

Alexander Toeldte, former CEO of Boise Inc. and current chairman of the board for Clearwater Paper, had this to say about capital expenditure analysis:

> One of the most important things for any economic analysis to work is the consistency of assumptions. I've had teams come to me to say, "We have two alternatives for this project. Alternative A looks attractive, but Alternative B is better because it has lower costs." Few people dig down into the details of the assumptions behind such recommendations. If you go through Alternative A, you might find they designed the asset with a stainless steel infrastructure, which has higher upfront costs but low maintenance costs. But when you go into the details of Alternative B, you might find an inconsistency buried in the footnotes, such as the team designing the asset using carbon steel instead of stainless. Carbon steel has lower

initial costs, but because it rusts, it will have to be repainted every year or so, driving up the long-term maintenance costs. These details make a difference: you cannot compare two analyses that have different fundamental assumptions.

This is important in any analysis, really. As a CEO, I wouldn't get involved with the details of the annual budgeting process. It's simply not the best use of the chief executive's time. Yet I would spend an entire day upfront discussing all the assumptions that went into the process. I would spend another day at the end of the process reviewing all the fundamental assumptions. In the interim, I directed the team that any changes in assumptions had to be discussed with and approved by me. This type of rigorous, disciplined approach is vital to any analysis and especially those involving capex strategy.

In most cases, one alternative tends to come out as a top contender, no matter what relevant sensitivities are thrown at it. As a matter of fact, we've seen some of the more extreme scenarios come to pass. In more than one instance, a company's CEO has found that not only was the new capex strategy still sound but it saved the company from certain disaster: if the original capex plan had been used, the company would have gone bankrupt. Instead, while its competitors were caught unawares, our client was able to substantially solidify the company's market position.

## COMPANY LIMITS AND LIMITATIONS

Finding the collection of strategic decisions that generates maximum cash flow is one thing. Figuring out whether the company can actually pursue that strategy is another. At this point, Superior Paper's team must ask if each of the candidates for the RfA is practically possible, considering current resources, financial restrictions, and customer expectations. Can it be funded without having to go to the capital markets? If not, might it make sense to finance the difference? Does it affect the ability to deliver on the company's dividend policy? The links into other capital allocation issues such as financing, dividend policies, and so on, are direct.

These issues are all potential limitations. A "limit" is a natural boundary. As far as we know, we cannot travel faster than the speed of light. That's a physical limit. A "limitation," on the other hand, is an artificial limit. Grammatically speaking, highway speed limits should be "speed limitations." We can physically exceed the posted speed, but we are legally restricted to it. In a perfect world (as far as strategy is concerned), there would be no limitations. Unfortunately, in the real world, there are plenty.

Our client teams face limitations all the time. As we covered, their allowed-for capex frames may not be sufficient. It could be that Superior Paper doesn't have the human resources available to manage all those changes, or perhaps the company doesn't have the balance sheet resources to carry out such an ambitious strategy.

A useful feature of our process is that the economic model can value the costs of those limitations down to the dollar. If Superior Paper didn't have the financial resources to support the most financially attractive alternative, the team might be forced to pursue its second-best strategic alternative (SA23). The accumulated discounted cash flow difference between the best alternative (SA24) and the second best (SA23) is the opportunity cost of not pursuing the bigger capex strategy. Superior Paper can calculate that restricting the capex budget to only allow for SA23 would cost the company $25 in lost opportunity.

There are also the limitations of nonproduction issues. Take the case of Christian Streiff, CEO of Airbus for all of three months. Part of his plan to save the company—by cutting $2 billion before it declined any further—was to "carousel" certain production units, such as moving the manufacture of the A380 from Hamburg to Toulouse. As the *New York Times* reported, ". . . officials in Berlin warned [Airbus] . . . not to make Germany bear the brunt of cutbacks . . . the German finance minister, Peer Steinbrück, [said], 'It's important to us that German factories be treated equally, in view of the current difficulties.'"*

We feel Streiff's pain. We have also seen a client's particularly promising SA shelved because of such political considerations, costing its shareholders billions of dollars in unrealized economic value creation over the decades to come

Again, the economic model allows companies to figure out exactly how much that decision costs by comparing the ideal SA against the strategy they are being forced to pursue. If the board believed that a closure would hurt the stock price or that acquiring Madrid would help it, the capex team could show the board how much each alternative would cost.

Superior Paper has its strategy, but it needs to create its capex plan. The project team wants to close London as quickly as possible, but its replacement production needs to come from somewhere. Using the capex strategy model, the team sees that it's better to debottleneck Frankfurt and Helsinki before closing London. Frankfurt's 100 kton debottleneck is relatively straightforward (compared to Helsinki's quality upgrade), so the team decides it should come first. Ideally, the Helsinki capacity would come online shortly before shuttering London, As such, the team expects that London will operate for another three years. Seven years after that will mark a decade of running Brussels for cash, after which it faces either a closure or a significant rebuild. The final result is a 50% increase in accumulated discounted cash flow and a 15% reduction in $CO_2$ emissions, with an option of either reinvesting or consolidating Brussels in the medium term.

---

* Landler, M., and N. Clark. "Airbus Chief of 3 Months Resigns Post." *New York Times*, October 10, 2006. https://www.nytimes.com/2006/10/10/business /worldbusiness/10airbus.html.

# 12

# EXECUTION

After potentially hundreds of strategic building blocks (SBBs) and strategic alternatives (SAs) have been created, analyzed, compared, and subjected to sensitivity analyses, one SA will emerge as the winner. Now, your team needs to translate this strategy into communicable and actionable steps. We offer three tips and tricks to do so when presenting the recommendation for action (RfA).

First, build a story in a presentation using graphs. (As mentioned earlier, we only tell these stories with accumulated discount cash flow curves.) How did the team arrive at the conclusions? How did it iterate its way forward to arrive at the RfA? Don't just present the selected SA, but also relevant SAs that did not qualify, and explain why. What sensitivities was the RfA subjected to? Most importantly, how much extra cash flow will this course of action bring? Also, explain the capex commitment and when the capital needs to be spent.

Second, form a concise RfA. It should comprise a step-by-step plan mapped against a timeline. When we say "concise," we mean it—our RfAs fit on one presentation slide. Skip the details; focus on the where, what, and when. Summarize the total effect from the perspectives of accumulated discounted cash flow value, EBITDA, and sustainability.

For Superior Paper, its RfA might look something like this:

- Start prestudy to expand Frankfurt +100 ktons ASAP; execute and plan to be up and running by year two.
- Start prestudy to debottleneck and improve Helsinki +50 ktons ASAP; execute and plan to be up and running by year three.
- Prepare to close London and sell the property. Start moving products and customers to Frankfurt and Helsinki as soon as they're up and running. Execute closure in year three. Do not approve any capexes in London, except those strictly necessary to keep customers and maintain safe operations until the move.
- Run Brussels for cash, expecting an exit in year 10. Do not approve any capexes in Brussels except those strictly necessary to keep customers and maintain safe operations. Develop options for future growth or consolidation as the closure year approaches.
- Encourage Frankfurt and Helsinki to search for and develop capex opportunities with long paybacks of 8–10 years or longer.
- This comprehensive recommendation is endorsed by a unanimous capex committee. The committee arrived at this recommendation after developing 24 full-scale strategic alternatives and subjecting them to extensive sensitivity tests.
- The recommendation is expected to improve long-term accumulated discounted cash flows by almost $200M, raise the EBITDA margin by 5 percentage points, and significantly improve company sustainability (both from a profitability standpoint, and in regard to greenhouse emissions).
- Procrastinating on any part of this recommendation will hurt Superior Paper's value creation and competitiveness.

Third, create a "Do Not Do!" slide closely following the RfA slide. It should cover the SBBs from the analyses that always delivered bad results in SAs. Continuing with the case of Superior Paper, these soundbites might say:

- Do not buy Madrid.
- In London, do not invest anything beyond the absolute bare minimum to keep operations running safely, regardless of payback.
- Ignore Brussels' shorter paybacks.
- Do not prioritize Brussels' capexes over Frankfurt's and Helsinki's.

Fourth, create one slide per facility where you outline in more detail which SBBs have been developed for the facility, what the conclusions are in more detail, and what the approach should be regarding smaller-to-medium capexes in the facility. Here are some examples with Frankfurt and Brussels:

**Frankfurt:** Given the current assumptions, scope, and alternatives we looked into:

- In the base alternative, Frankfurt's accumulated discounted cash flow reaches a value of close to $90 million. Despite the assumed yearly margin decline, Frankfurt continues to generate positive cash flow for more than 20 years.
- The base alternative indicates that (from a stand-alone cash flow perspective) the re-investability in Frankfurt, as it is being run in the base, is better than the system average.

- Four strategic building blocks have been developed involving Frankfurt. The base alternative, Close, Debottleneck +70 units, Debottleneck +100 units
- Frankfurt performs well relative to its peers and alternatives where the mill is closed hurt the system.

Given the cash flow performance of Frankfurt, current assumptions, scope, alternatives considered, and sensitivities performed, Superior Paper should:

- Start prestudy to expand Frankfurt +100 ktons ASAP; execute and plan to be up and running by year two.
- Qualify customers and move volumes, mainly from London
- Run Frankfurt, expecting it to still operate beyond 20 years from now.

- Actively search for and encourage investment opportunities, even with relatively long paybacks (five to six years).

**Brussels:** Given the current assumptions, scope and alternatives investigated:

- In the base alternative, Brussel's cash flow accumulated generation reaches just above $50 million.
- The base alternative indicates that (from a standalone cash flow perspective) the "re-investability" in Brussels, as it is being run in the base alternative, is relatively low.

- Three strategic building blocks have been developed involving Brussels: the base alternative, Close, Debottleneck +25 units.

Given the cash flow performance of Brussels, current assumptions, scope, alternatives considered, and sensitivities performed, Superior Paper should:

- Run Brussels for cash, expecting an exit in year 10. Do not approve any capexes in Brussels except those strictly necessary to keep customers and maintain safe operations.
- Do not accept any payback-motivated capexes. That capital is better spent elsewhere.
- Develop options for future growth or consolidation as the closure year approaches.

Once the company moves forward with this RfA, leadership must go a step further so that this isn't a one-time project but becomes a new way of operating.

# GOVERNANCE

Superior Paper doesn't need to replace its current capital budgeting process, as such. Rather, our process provides an added dimension; an overlay of the company's current approach to capex management and capital budgeting. The short- to medium-term capex process works more or less in the same way, no matter what company, industry, or country you go to:

1. Capital Budgeting (time frame: one to three years)
   - Gather capex needs and opportunities from the organization.

- Prioritize and rank.
- Approve total capex budget (often an arbitrary amount based on history or even depreciation levels).
- Follow up on the capex budget during the year and reallocate capital as needed due to unforeseen events.

**2.** Capex Process (day-to-day operations)
- Submit actual request and route through various checkpoints and analyze.
- Base decisions on key performance indicators and if there is room in budget.
- Execute capex and follow up on outlays. Follow up on capex projects to determine if the decision delivered the promised results in a postcompletion review.

This process is visually depicted in Figure 12.1.

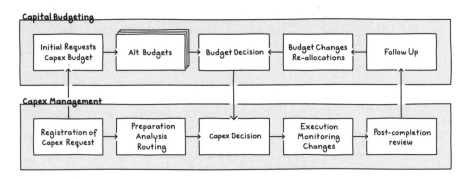

The process works from a pure control and administrative point of view, but it needs strategic steering: Where should capital be allocated? In what businesses and sites should it be invested? What should be done now versus 5 or 10 years from now? How much should be allocated? In most companies, the process just described is a tail that wags the dog; it's putting the cart before the horse. Having a proper capex strategy is what turns this around, putting both animals in their rightful roles.

Figure 12.2 visually adds a proper capex strategy layer to the overall capex process.

The RfA in the capex strategy is what dictates which capex needs and opportunities are included in the capex budget, and ultimately what decisions are made. The capex strategy sets the rules for what sites get to invest, and under which conditions (not the individual capex projects' payback, NPV, or IRR). The budget and capex process go from being a piecemeal ranking process to being the vehicle of the strategy.

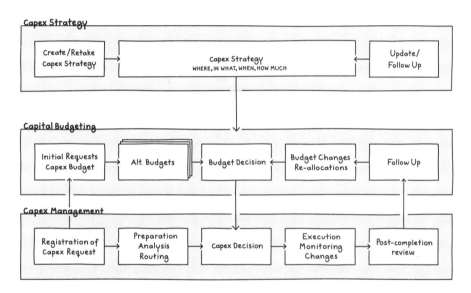

Take the Brussels mill in Superior Paper as an example. The recommendation is to run that mill for cash. That means that no capex should be approved based on a capex payback rationale. On the other hand, Frankfurt will be around for many decades to come. Here, the company should encourage initiatives to further its competitiveness, even if the capex payback may be long. It's not uncommon for our clients to find that a sound capex project may have a payback stretching more than 10 years; whatever improvements we make here will be harvested for a very long time.

With this mindset, Frankfurt will keep getting better and better, and will therefore not end up being a C mill for many decades to come.

Understanding that the capex strategy governs the day-to-day decisions in the capex process enables executives to understand that the value of the budget and management process does not come from its ability to rank and put individual requests against each other. Rather, it comes from the process's ability to enforce the strategy principles throughout the organization, to facilitate good governance, and to enable learning.

To fully benefit from a capex strategy, the company needs a way to enforce its vision in the day-to-day. Up until recently, the choice for digital tools for handling a capital allocation process has been lacking. But now there is no excuse; purpose-built tools now exist to facilitate these processes. We include our own SaaS solution in this lineup, integrating the capex strategy into the traditional process as a governing layer. The latest breed of purpose-built capex SaaS solutions significantly improve governance, transparency, accountability, and overall efficiency. Perhaps more importantly, they enable companies to benefit from the large pool of valuable data that is created both before, and in the follow-up of, decisions.

The tight integration to the capex strategy ensures that instead of the capital budget being driven by capex needs and arbitrary figures, it is now based on maximizing the cash flow from a production portfolio. A challenge that leadership may face is to continuously communicate to the board the idea that the promised value is based on the strategy working as a whole. Some board members may ask for the delta of the individual decisions, and these may not look good, even if they are a vital part of overall strategy. It is up to leadership to help these board members change their perspective, from looking at capex as an analytical problem to seeing it as an interconnected system. This is a learning process for the board, too, as Annica Bresky, president and CEO, Stora Enso, explains in the Afterword.

## Perpetuating the Cycle

In many companies—indeed, in many industries—there's a lack of trust between the owners, or boards of directors, and leadership. This stems from leadership's continual promises to generate shareholder value and continued inability to substantially fulfill that promise. As a result of this, the board is often reluctant to approve a capex budget beyond what is strictly necessary. Leadership has learned to put forth only the capexes that offer the highest returns (however that's measured) with the quickest paybacks. As we've demonstrated, those projects obscure capex opportunities and notably distort true performance, leading to resources allocated away from the best businesses and directed toward the worst. This simply perpetuates the destructive practice of running the production portfolio according to the going concern principle, and again the tail wags the dog.

In some cases, this has resulted in professionals going so far as to see capex as a necessary evil—something to be avoided at all costs until it simply cannot be ignored any longer, a company penalty. The truth is, there are virtually always substantial capital allocation opportunities in production portfolios just waiting to be discovered.

The capex strategy should be "owned" by a capex strategy committee that updates the capex strategy economic model every year (or more frequently) with actual numbers from the capex projects implemented, as well as with updated market demand, costs, and so on. The base alternative is updated, the SBBs are updated, and the SAs are then automatically updated. Carousels are updated with new prices, manufacturing costs, freight costs, and demand assumptions. New SBBs are developed because the team keeps being creative and new business opportunities arise. New SAs are created to see if the strategy can be further improved.

As needed, the committee adjusts the capex plan as decisions are made about which capexes to fund and when, as well as with additional opportunities. In this way, Superior Paper's strategy is always based on the most updated data and the most accurate projections—and always the best way into the future for the company.

The capex strategy process will also be ready to deal with sudden events such as a significant competitor's move, a large demand drop, a devastating facility fire, and so on. The company can move to again update data, create new SBBs, and make new combinations. Superior Paper will always be ready, even in the face of the unforeseeable.

# PART III

# Capex as an Economic Catalyst

# 13

# SUSTAINABLE DESTRUCTION

More people on Earth have access to running water than ever before, both in absolute numbers and per capita. More have access to some form of healthcare than ever before. More have access to education . . . to electricity . . . to financing. More people are globally connected than ever before. The cost of personal hygiene products has plummeted, allowing more people to afford basic necessities. The cost of computing power has dropped and technology access has risen, allowing people from all corners of the world to compete with their peers from developed nations. The cost of renewable energy is rapidly falling. The technology to harness renewable energy sources is not only cheaper but far more widespread than just two decades ago.

We're not ignoring the inherent problems that still exist, there will be conflict and natural disasters. We don't see the world through rose-colored glasses. We're merely pointing out that the median quality of life for the global population has risen by nearly any measure we wish to examine—thanks, in large part, to capex.

In earlier chapters, we spoke about systems thinker Dr. W. Edwards Deming. You can't mention Deming without talking about Japan's economic recovery after World War II. As

Japan rebuilt from the rubble, virtually all of its manufacturing infrastructure was brand new. No wonder its economic growth skyrocketed in the following decades. By the early nineties, however, Japan hit the wall, as growth no longer could be achieved simply by adding new and better things, or by working with continuous improvement. The country's industrial sector had matured, requiring creative destruction (i.e., planned closures and exits) for the benefit of expansion and growth in different locations or in different parts of the economy. Creative destruction is a virtuous cycle, but it's a cycle that must continue to spin.

Globally, our clients' sustained increase in annual cash flows due to adopting a wiser way to allocate capital currently stands at $8 billion. For comparison, that's 1.5% of Sweden's entire annual economic output—and this, from working with only dozens of clients around the world. Clearly, our estimates can be debated, and our calculations undoubtedly contain some errors. Regardless, the impact of a superior approach to capex strategy has been undeniably substantial.

We can't take the credit, of course. Ultimately, these decisions are made and carried out by our clients. Our process merely provides them a better lens to identify and capitalize on the capital allocation opportunities already existing within their production portfolios.

A strategy may provide direction, but execution is everything.

## WHY DESTRUCTION IS GOOD

For the kind of progress we've been talking about to occur, better methods and technologies must continually replace the outdated ones—both at the micro scale (such as upgrading an extruder) and at the macro scale (such as building a new production facility while closing an obsolete one).

Sometimes it's easy to see the micro-level impact of a capex decision. Take, for instance, a greenfield site that creates hundreds of new jobs and the millions of dollars that go to vendors, suppliers, contractors, and others. But what about the broader impact that we can't easily see? What about the taxes generated from increased cash flows that fund public schools and libraries, public healthcare, and public infrastructure? What about the social programs supported by the value created from these sites' taxes? What about the local and national programs funded by these additional public revenues? What about the multiplier effect on local economies?

As mentioned in Chapter 1, consider the fact that more than 20% of the average country's economy is composed of fixed capital formation (private plus public capital allocation). That is, one-fifth of any given nation's economy is driven by capital allocation decisions. Imagine if, like Japan in the 1950s, all of a country's major companies were just slightly better at investing capital. The cumulative effects—like Japan by the 1960s—would be astonishing. Literally world changing.

We've not yet mentioned the beneficial environmental impact of creative destruction. Better methods and superior technologies reduce material input and throughput, translating into less waste, less or better utilized by-products, less energy, lower $CO_2$ emissions, and a smaller overall company footprint. Superior gross domestic product growth further allows for the financing of new and better technologies. Some might see us as "techno-optimists," but our perspective comes from our direct experience in tracking environmental costs and impacts as part of clients' capex strategy analyses. One of our clients is, in fact, carbon *negative*. (Of course, it helps that the client is one of the largest private owner of forestland in Europe.) While climate change is a much broader issue, we're proud that our clients are a part of the solution.

> At the heart of capitalism is creative destruction.
> —Joseph Schumpeter

Creative destruction creates value as a consequence of market forces; companies are forced to do more with less. We had a three-site project once that led to a consolidation of the sites into one with a new brownfield. That single mill now produces more volume than the original three combined and operates at a multiple of the industry's average competitiveness. In other instances, we've worked with integrated pulp and paper mills that burn their wood by-products to create electricity for the local grid. The mills generate the equivalent of a small nuclear power plant yet are powered by a renewable resource. If that's not progress, we don't know what is. In our experience, the results are unequivocal—superior capex strategies create substantial economic and environmental value. Maximizing long-term shareholder value is good for the company, the country, and Mother Nature. At least, that's been the result for our clients over about the past 25 years.

If creative destruction is a good thing, as we believe and have experienced it to be, then the questions become: How do we get more of it? How do we speed up the process? The answer is that it is difficult. The creative destruction funnel is a result of free-market forces at play. They determine how quickly the twin factors of increasing input costs and decreasing cost of finished goods move. What we can do, individually and organizationally, is remove the barriers that would slow these forces down.

## GROWTH AMBITIONS AS BARRIERS TO CREATIVE DESTRUCTION

As we've indicated, growth isn't a good goal for relatively mature companies in relatively mature industries.* If it's achieved, it should be the result of an effective capex strategy; a means to an end, not an end unto itself. For example, imagine Superior Paper's CEO had the aim to grow by 5% in all markets. The company could have far surpassed that goal by acquiring the Madrid site. The company would have grown from 845 units to more than 1,000—a 23% increase.

---

* As we noted earlier, this could look different in the very early stages of establishing a market as in the life of a startup.

Yet company cash flow would have remained virtually unchanged in the short term and would have decreased over the long term. The transaction would have created zero economic value, despite substantially growing the top line. Moreover, growth ambitions not founded in a sound value creating capex strategy often slow down or completely halt the willingness of executives to proactively handle the creative destruction funnel. The results include investing in, and sometimes even expanding, C mills; being led into bad acquisitions; underinvesting in sound assets; and more.

## DECLINING MARKETS AS A BARRIER TO CREATIVE DESTRUCTION

Several of our clients have been partially, or in some cases completely, in businesses that are in a demand decline from a volume and market perspective. Newsprint is a good example. Declining markets, however, are never an excuse to stop searching for the right place to add capacity. The trick is still, as always, to find where to consolidate and where to expand. It is not unusual that we find individual speed-ups in the best of sites that, from a value point of view, are worth more than keeping several other sites, even if the ratio of volumes added is as much as 1:10 compared to what is closed. We claim that companies' inability to find both expansion and consolidation opportunities does extra harm when operating in declining markets. It is then extra important to find ways of removing barriers to the creative destruction process—to be ahead of the demand drop curve instead of continuously trailing it.

## POLITICAL BARRIERS TO CREATIVE DESTRUCTION

Then there are the economic restrictions that slow the forces of creative destruction. For example, we've seen green credits in the

European Union that result in preserving old industrial sites, rather than allowing them to be challenged by better facilities elsewhere. Old pulp mills in Europe get green credits for installing brand-new boilers that burn wood chips to produce power in a more environmentally friendly way. For every kilowatt hour that the mill sends to the region's power grid, it gets a certain amount of money from the country's government (that is, directly from public funds). Essentially, many older—and pollution-generating—sites are effectively subsidized by the state. Without green credits to invest in, say, a new boiler like this or a state-of-the-art turbine, there'd be no way to justify keeping the site open.

From our experience, it seems that punishing the unwanted behavior (e.g., taxing carbon emissions) is an accelerant for closing the worst performers and making room for better ones. This is especially true when it comes to polluted sites. We know of one industrial site that has terrible cash flow, aging equipment, and a layout that was antiquated 20 years ago. Why does its parent company keep the site in operation? Because the minute the company decides to close the plant, it will trigger all of the environmental cleanup costs (which amount to a staggering figure—*well* into the hundreds of millions of dollars). Because of how environmental policy is written in that country, the company is incentivized to keep running an awful site with serious pollution issues. The better route might be to do what nuclear power plants usually need to do: start funding the costs of environmental cleanup years or even decades in advance. By the time the site is obsolete and ready for closure, its environmental outlays are already fully funded.

In the European Union, green credits have been distributed by country and by sites. If a company had four mills close together— say, Cologne, Rotterdam, Antwerp, and Luxembourg—a sound capex strategy analysis would probably find that more economic value could be created by combining all four sites into one new greenfield. However, despite the four European countries all being part of the European Economic Area, the emission rights don't transfer between them. This is effectively a self-defeating policy, considering it runs counter to the very spirit of the trade bloc's free movement of goods, people, services, and capital across borders.

Tariffs operate similarly. In effect, they subsidize goods manufactured with older, less efficient technology and methods. The public must spend more money on inferior goods, rather than purchase better ones more cheaply from suppliers abroad. The government's aim (ostensibly) is to protect its own national industries, but all it results in is destroying economic value for its people.

Contrary to what some of the public believes, some CEOs recognize how vital free trade is to business and nations. These forward-thinking leaders do *not* want tariffs for their line of business. Deming once wrote, "Nothing can do you so much harm as a lousy competitor. Be thankful for a good competitor."* Daniel was once an observer in a closed-door policy meeting of a prominent US national trade industry. The CEO of one the largest and most widely respected companies in the industry spoke out on behalf of not only his company, but for the private equity investment group that owned it: "We're not pro-tariff. We don't think it's good for our industry and we don't think it's good for the country."

In addition to economic policies, there are plenty of other national policies that impede creative destruction. Take the controlled economy of the former Soviet Union, for example. Its economic system didn't allow for free market forces. Industrial output was dictated by government officials. Prices were regulated, so the all-important declining margins that push for creative destruction did not exist. We believe we can make the case that this was one of the major contributing factors to its eventual collapse. Value was constantly being destroyed without a proportional amount of value being created.

Something similar has happened in China: its one-party government is trying to control its economy. The government issues mandates based, largely or at least in part, on political ideology

---

* Deming, W. Edwards. *The New Economics for Industry, Government, Education, Third Edition*. Cambridge, MA: MIT Press, 2018.

instead of allowing companies to respond to free market forces. The more it does this, the slower its creative destruction. If it continues on its current course, Chinese industries will never be competitive enough to catch up with their competitors operating in countries that experience faster creative destruction cycles. While China may gain some ground, we posit that it will never catch up to a per capita basis until its government moves closer toward real capitalism and free markets, and freedom of speech is of course a keystone ingredient in operating not only a nation well but also a company. No company that gags its staff works well in the long run. We anticipate that China will experience a similar growth pattern as Japan: full speed ahead to "partially" catch up and then stall.

If countries want value creation, they should allow the mechanism to gain more economic destruction to play out.

## CULTURAL BARRIERS TO CREATIVE DESTRUCTION

We've used Deming's thinking as examples throughout this book, which leads us to the questions: Why did Japan's economy start stagnating in the 1990s? What changed from 20 years earlier when its growth was the envy of the world?

After the war, Japan's economic infrastructure was devastated. Close to 90% of its factories, utilities, and public transportation networks had been reduced to rubble. Its industrial base had to be built from the ground up in the 1950s and 1960s.

The forces of creative destruction lead to producing more with less. To casual observers, a factory closing is a bad sign. They may assume the company is in financial trouble, the market has dropped, or the site was mismanaged, or make any number of negative assumptions. Take the London example. The mill had the highest EBITDA margins of any of the four sites and contributed more cash flow than the other three. It was a healthy mill. Without the lens of systems thinking, outside observers are left scratching their heads, wondering why Superior Paper would close a perfectly good mill. No matter how the company presents it, people will assume something went wrong.

In general, the perception is that Japanese companies are even more concerned with outward appearances than their Western counterparts. For many Japanese CEOs, closing a Japanese production site is a nonstarter, regardless of what it contributes to or costs the company's portfolio.

Culturally, a country's citizens must be more accepting of the types of rapid changes required by creative destruction. There are countries where local governments and unions team up to stop companies from shutting production sites, and we know for a fact that some companies actively avoid investing in those countries. In the long run, these attitudes are impediments to further value creation. This is why we firmly believe that creative destruction works best in a country where a strong support for capitalism and free markets is coupled with strong social programs, to make it easier for people to handle the abrupt shocks and mitigate the short-term adverse effects. In our view, this is *real* capitalism, where no resource—and especially not persons—should perform at anything but peak potential.

## PERSONAL BARRIERS TO CREATIVE DESTRUCTION

Then there are some CEOs who don't focus on maximizing long-term value creation—at least, not the company's. We remember one project where some members of the steering team were reluctant to even consider moving production from one particular site, despite its obvious dismal performance. When we pressed them, we were told informally that on the other end of the site's large tract of land sat a fabulous cabin—the CEO's perfect getaway. He loved it so much we weren't allowed to even propose a strategic alternative that included shuttering the mill. It would have been a lot better to close the site and move the cabin, but the CEO was unwilling to for personal reasons. The CEO is now gone, and the site eventually (and inevitably) closed. In a market economy, these forces can be postponed but not stopped.

In another instance, a CEO wouldn't hear of a strategic alternative that involved shutting down two plants. Just before engaging with us, the CEO had pushed the board of directors to acquire the two sites. He felt it would be embarrassing to then back a plan that would consolidate the two into an existing site. We think the shareholders would have preferred the cash.

## INSTITUTIONAL BARRIERS TO CREATIVE DESTRUCTION

Creative destruction is a fundamental fact of free markets and capitalism, and the fundamental drivers of creative destruction are innovation and capital allocation. The smoother the wheels of the creative destruction process can turn, the higher the economic growth.* Any company serious about being part of creating future growth needs to foster a culture and mindset that acknowledges this fundamental fact and, further, embraces it. From our years of experience in this field—having worked in companies and countries that are more or less successful from this perspective—we have boiled down the main success factors to a few items.

From a mindset perspective:

- Allocating the owner's capital (through capex, acquisitions, and dividends) is *the* number one task of leadership.
- The decision makers in the organization need to be taught, and buy into, the fundamental concepts of holistic capital allocation and creative destruction.

---

* This does not mean that it does not come at a cost. Labor, for instance, does not move as easily between industries and geographies as capital does. Not addressing that on a political level may slow the economic wheels because it creates ethical, personal, and often political barriers to change.

- For facilities that may be closed within the next 5 to 10 years, leadership should remove, to the degree possible, any organizational, cultural, and lump-sum costs (such as environmental or contractual poison pills, etc.) and barriers to exit sites and businesses.
- Exits and closures do not equal failure.
- Leadership should foster an environment where the creation of large step-change options with long paybacks are encouraged.
- Capital funding is not scarce for the right projects. Good, credible, and long-term value creating projects—*that's* what is scarce.
- Leadership should not rely on or lobby for political "help" to slow the creative destruction process, such as import tariffs, and so on.* Instead, leaders should work to remove these.

From an organizational perspective:

- Leadership should create an "institution"—a capex strategy committee with the overall responsibility to create, maintain, challenge, and update the capex strategy going forward.
- Leadership should tie the day-to-day budgeting and capex management processes to its capex strategy process.
- Those who work with capex should have access to purpose-built software tools to ensure validity, consistency, transparency, and learning from and throughout the entire capital allocation process, from forming the strategy to the follow-ups for individual capex projects.

Mindset is the most important. This is where the difference truly is made. However, without the company institutionalizing it, such benefits are fleeting. Leadership can establish a mindset

* Destructive and strategic "dumping" of prices should and, of course, need to be addressed. That is not the same as artificially protecting weak industries.

through training and individual projects, but leaders will not maintain it and it won't live up to its potential if it is not systemized.

## CAPEX AS A CATALYST FOR CREATIVE DESTRUCTION

Whatever we may think about economic growth, climate change, inequality, and opportunity, you can be sure that what will most determine what the future looks like is how we allocate our resources: labor, land, water, raw materials, capital, and so on. While laws and regulations may provide a framework to operate within and public sentiment may provide direction, it's the hard decisions behind capital allocation that drive action.

If humankind is to experience progress, if everyone is to benefit from that progress, if we hope to increase the average person's quality of life while simultaneously living up to our environmental responsibilities to each other, and if we want to accomplish all this in way that's sustainable—socially, financially, economically, and environmentally—for the generations to come, we must become better at capital allocation. The margin for error has become extremely thin. If a fifth of the world's capital continues to be driven by poor capital allocation processes such as individual cash flow delta calculations, whether that be in regard to cash flow or $CO_2$ emissions, we'll have to wait long for the hoped-for progress. The world is nowhere near its full economic potential because of how terrible we collectively are at capital allocation—"a train wreck," as John Williams wrote in the Foreword.

On the other hand, we've witnessed firsthand how quickly companies can transform themselves to be aligned with the forces of creative destruction. The sustainable value these companies create—again, socially, financially, economically, and environmentally—is staggering. We're not pessimistic about the future, quite the opposite.

We say: "What an opportunity!"

# AFTERWORD

There is one thing this book has not touched on yet—putting your new capex strategy into action. In other words, this is the change management piece. Once the consultants leave, all the work to be done falls on the shoulders of those left behind. I've been one of those people who had to manage the aftermath of Daniel and Fredrik coming into a company four times now.

The first time, I was the manager of a mill at a challenged site. Being in charge of a facility where you're basically being told, "You're going to run for cash and then possibly close," is quite an experience. The second and third times, I was responsible for a business area, and then an entire division. Those had their challenges, to be sure. But I face some of the biggest challenges in my role as president and CEO of the Finnish company Stora Enso, one of the largest wood products, pulp, and packaging companies in the world.

Being at these four different levels of leadership has provided me with a perspective I think few can appreciate without having been through it personally. Weissenrieder & Co. hasn't written a change management book yet, but I wish it would. In each position, I was in uncharted waters; there was no manual to guide me through the day-to-day reality of navigating in the wake of Daniel and Fredrik's (creative) destruction. I was delighted when they asked if I would share what I've learned.

Fredrik talks about the mood of the capex project team throughout an ongoing project. He warns the team that in the middle of it, there comes a point when you'll feel depressed and worn down. "But don't worry about the confusion, it'll clear up in just a bit and the conclusions will make you feel better!" He's right. The team does achieve clarity and the conclusions usually make you feel better . . . but with a kind of sobering, concrete clarity. There's no question about what needs to be done. What's left is how you handle your people and the courage you need as a leader to execute the plan.

In all four of my roles, I've found transparency is key. It was quite a shock when it became clear to me that my mill had been classified as a challenged mill. How do you communicate to a local leadership team that the mill is going to be run for cash for a couple of years and then possibly closed? How do you tell 500 people that our job is now to generate as much cash as possible and that no one is going to invest in us anymore? But you have to tell them. You have to think about the impact of these things on your people and the local societies where that kind of news travels fast. In many locations, such mills are the single employers in the area. Closing down that site can have serious social implications.

I assembled all the shifts, all the managers, and everyone in the office, and then I told them face-to-face exactly what was happening. I didn't hide it. I didn't try to sugarcoat it. And I had a wonderful team at that mill. After a few days of shock, many workers and managers came to my office with basically the same message: "We are resilient." "We are fighters!" "We will not give up our mill this easily." "Let's show them what we can do." So, we all decided that we were going to show corporate we were better than they believed.

The mill united for a common cause; we broke a lot of the "us and them" mentality that was there between management and workers or between different parts of the organization. Everyone was committed and contributed. We put our heads together and came up with creative ways to improve productivity without any capex investments from corporate. We revamped our product portfolio. We looked at workflows and processes. We found better ways of doing things here and there. The local politicians and community pulled together to support us. This became a core part of the culture at that mill that continued long after I left. I am thrilled to say that, because of the "new culture" and innovations everyone found, that mill survived and is still running today, almost 15 years later. So, even when things are dark, there is hope.

In my upper management roles, I had to be clear about what it means to be a leadership team. You are simply there to prioritize and make sure the resources of the company, be it cash or the efforts of the people, are spent wisely. Because many of them were part of the process, they could see for themselves what needed to be done.

Through that, they didn't defend their own areas of responsibilities and their own businesses but agreed that the health and future of our company were more important. But for some leaders it was impossible to change their mindsets and they had to leave the team. Another consequence I also had to consider is the different ways leaders are incentivized. Their individual performances and their bonuses should not be set counter to the capex strategy and, therefore, what's best for the company. By disconnecting incentives from local performance, you weren't penalized if you generated ideas that could result in a future reduction of your own business.

For those who weren't part of the project team, I did a couple of sessions. I shared insights upfront and prepared them for what they may encounter. I walked them through what I had experienced and seen for myself. I communicated my expectations, and I brought in other leaders to share their perspectives, too. That made it easier for my other managers to adopt the mentality of "Let's do what's best for the company. We're not here to defend our own turf." That kind of transparency is important for change management in general and crucial for the level of change we'd decided upon.

It's also a bit of a curse when you find your A mills. Suddenly, there are a lot of capexes thrown at it that require a lot of effort to implement. Sometimes you have to change people to be able to move at a much quicker pace. Or you will need different competencies in leadership in order to effect these changes that need to take place.

Lastly, becoming a CEO brought an additional new challenge: getting buy-in from the board. Many board members' perspectives aren't about investing in your best assets, as you might intuitively think. They have also been brought up with the nonsystemic capex allocation. Their view might be: How can we save the C mills? How can we get them up to par with the A and B mills and improve their performance? Or they don't always want to take the difficult decisions that cause bad press and publicity, preferring rather to keep these older assets running, pouring money into poor performers because they believe that's what they need to do.

It's difficult to bring people into the type of thinking that things are born, they mature, and eventually they die, whether it's a site, a technology, or a product. The company, however, always has to move forward. You can't be stuck trying to save the past and invest in the future at the same time. You have to let some things go so you can invest in the products or technologies of the future.

For my board, I've run mini-education sessions to communicate why we needed a different approach, ultimately leading to investments in our strategic sites but also the closures of two sites: "It's going to cost this, but if we continue running them, it will consume our capital investment budget and make us forgo these other opportunities." I've had Daniel and Fredrik give presentations to help the board understand why IRR on individual capex requests was no longer the way we viewed capital allocation and that the holistic capex strategy now would determine that.

Then, as with any change project, there's the challenge of making it stick. Otherwise, this will be seen as a project. When a new CEO comes in, he or she will throw everything out and start all over. So, it's quite important to internalize and make it part of the culture. I work closely with my CFO and head of strategy, the business leaders, and our finance community. Together, we set the governance structures, performance follow-up systems, and capex allocation forums. We are all responsible for keeping this new way of thinking alive at Stora Enso. We have a structured way of seeing our company and our cash flow opportunities. It's not something that we did once but something we do every year, continually updating our lists to match our progress of implementation. That's how we make it stick—it becomes part of the culture of the company.

Not just a new way of doing but a new way of thinking.

**Annica Bresky**
President and CEO, Stora Enso

# ACKNOWLEDGMENTS

We owe so many people thanks, both personally and professionally. When it comes to the content and creation of this book, we would like to specifically name:

Erik Ottosson: In 1994, you and Fredrik developed the foundation of what would become the process presented in this book. If it weren't for you, our company wouldn't exist today.

Martin Wengblad: You did more than business development—you were instrumental in communicating our consultancy's and our process's value. The two of us are grateful for all your work.

Håkan Tengberg and Robert Kongs: In the late 1990s, you two began working with us and Erik to create our proprietary software tool, Weissr®. You have been the backbone of the IT operations of our company and our software, continually improving productivity, security, usability, and every conceivable facet of technology. Thanks to you and the rest of the team in Riga.

Ole Terland, senior vice president of strategy, SCA: Thank you for your critical evaluation of our manuscript and, more importantly, your genuine support for our work and efforts over the decades.

Toby Lawton, CFO, SCA: Thank you for your feedback on the manuscript from the perspective of a (brilliant) financial professional.

Olivia Romero Lejonthun, Herengracht Studios: Thank you for creating all the illustrations herein.

Annica Bresky, president & CEO, Stora Enso: Thank you for letting your words serve as the perfect Afterword and for your genuine support for our work and efforts over the years.

John Williams, president & CEO, Domtar: Thank you for your great comments on the shape and flow of the manuscript, for writing the Foreword, and for being one of our biggest advocates over our journey together through two organizations.

Alexander Toeldte, executive chairman, board of Clearwater Paper Corporation: Thank you for your thorough, page-by-page evaluation of the manuscript's contents and concepts. Every single one of your edits and suggestions were addressed.

Steve Scherger, EVP & CFO, Graphic Packaging International: Thank you for reviewing our draft from the perspective of the CFO of a Fortune 500 company.

Cynthia Zigmund, literary agent, Second City Publishing: Thank you for seeing the potential of our book even in its infancy, for so ably representing us, and for finding our book a home at McGraw Hill .

Stephen Isaacs and Judith Newlin, senior editors, McGraw Hill Professional: Thank you, Stephen, for wanting to publish our book before there even was a book; congratulations on your retirement. Thank you, Judith, for a graceful transition as you "inherited" us from your predecessor and for shepherding us through McGraw Hill 's publication process.

Derek Lewis, business book collaborator: When we first reached out to you for help on our book in 2020, we had no idea that this would be the result. You have guided us through the process and added much value.* Thank you.

Our clients: Our approach to capex strategy came from being by your side in the trenches, working on the everyday reality of capital allocation decisions. Thank you for your faith and confidence in our ability to help your company reach its full potential.

Our team: A heartfelt thanks to all the professionals at Weissenrieder & Co.

---

\* Accumulated discounted cash flow value

# INDEX

Accumulated discounted cash flow curves, 4, 102–113, 151, 185

Accumulated discounted cash flows, 102–113

Acquisitions, 78, 165, 172–175

Action matrix, 170, 171*t*

Airbus, 183–184

"Airbus Chief of 3 Months Resigns" (Landler and Clark), 183–184

Alternative capex strategies: comparing, 74–75, 108, 147

AM (asset mapping), 99, 115 (*See also* Strategic asset mapping for base alternative))

American Automobile Association (AAA), 7

Analytic thinking, 10, 29–30, 173

Annuity depreciation, 53

A sites:
   categorization of, 26–27
   investing in, 37, 38*t*, 65
   management attention for, 39–40, 40*t*
   production volume and cash flow of, 38–39

Assessment, capex strategy model for, 122

Asset base, 79

Asset mapping (AM), 99, 115 (*See also* Strategic asset mapping for base alternative)

Assets:
   capital intensity and, 85
   determining value of, 165
   interdependencies between markets and, 101–102
   life cycle of, 36–37, 52
   operational age of, 132–133
   payback period and age of, 22
   strategic asset mapping for new, 133–135
   underperforming, 25
   useful lifespan of, 34–35, 135–136
   variable costs of, 142

Assumptions of capex strategy model:
   about capex growth, 120, 125
   about EBITDA margins, 120, 125–128
   about equal treatment of production sites, 120, 123–124
   about market price, 120, 128–129
   about product mix, 120, 124–125
   about strategic intent, 120, 123
   and base alternative, 120, 123–129
   consistency of, 181–182

Automation, of quality control, 71

BA (*see* Base alternative)
Backward-looking performance measures, 46–47
Balance-sheet based profitability measures, 46, 47–53
Bankruptcy, 73
Base alternative (BA):
  assumptions about, 120, 123–129
  for capex strategy model, 115–120
  cash flows for, 141–151
  creating, 115–129
  and EBITDA margins, 125–128
  and growing capex needs, 125
  and market-based internal pricing, 128–129
  performing below company's, 150
  and production, 124–125
  special treatment of, 123–124
  strategic asset mapping for, 131–139
  strategic intent and, 123
  in timelines for capex strategies, 99
Baseball, systems thinking in, 10–13
Base year cash flows, 143–145
Beane, Billy, 10–13, 33
Berkshire Hathaway, 42–43
Better-than-average leadership, 7
Boise Cascade, 181
Bresky, Annica, 75, 158, 192
B sites:
  categorization of, 26–27
  investing in, 37–38, 38t, 65
  management attention for, 40, 40t
Budgets for capital expenditures, 3–27
  bad process for creating, 66–67
  based on categorization of sites, 37, 65
  and cash flow deltas, 18–21
  and investing in aging assets/poorly-performing sites, 21–27

as long-term strategy, 88–89
and metrics for value of capex projects, 13–18
project performance and cash flow, 3–9
systems thinking about, 9–13
Buffet, Warren, 42–43
Buisson-Street, Guillum, 155n*
Buy backs, share, 76

Calculations, in capex strategy model, 121
Capacity closures, 162
Capex (*see* Capital expenditures)
Capex budgets (*see* Budgets for capital expenditures)
Capex delta, calculations of, 180
Capex management, 190f, 191f
Capex needs:
  assumptions about growth of, 120, 125
  BA to identify, 123
  as drivers of capital allocation, 13
  and EBITDA multiples, 172–173
  predicting future, 173–174
  proactive approach to, 8
  as systemic sensitivity, 178
Capex process, 190, 190f
Capex strategies:
  for capital allocation, 122
  comparing alternative, 74–75, 108, 147
  to discover opportunities for capital allocation, 90
Capex strategy committee, 193–194
Capex strategy model, 115–129
  and accumulated discounted cash flows/curves, 102–113
  assumptions in, 123–129
  and base alternatives, 115–120
  cash flows for base alternative in, 141–151
  collecting data for, 98
  company team for, 94–97

core principles for, 93–114
creating, 115–129
example, 117–120
overview of, 121–122
phases of, 115
RfAs to implement, 185–194
scope and managerial control of,
    100–102
sensitivity tests in, 177–182
strategic alternatives in, 163–175
strategic asset mapping of base
    alternative for, 131–139
strategic building blocks for,
    153–162
testing, 146–150
timeline for, 98–100
Capital allocation, 69–90
beyond shareholder value, 81–83
capex needs/opportunities as
    drivers of, 13
capex strategy to discover
    opportunities for, 90
capex *vs.*, 75–84
and capital intensity, 84–90
as driver of creative destruction,
    206
economy driven by, 199
and growth in manufacturing,
    79–81
improving efficiency of, 9–13
in markets with higher added
    value products, 77–78
measuring, 80–81
progress driven by, 208
as reason companies exist, 83–84
and resource allocation, 69–70
and shareholder value, 81
for value creation, 69–75
Capital assets, capital intensity and,
    85
Capital budgeting, 189–190, 190*f*,
    191*f*
Capital costs, 178
Capital expenditures (capex):

accounting for future, 172–173
analysis of, 181–182
broad impact of, 199
capital allocation and, 13, 75–84
as catalyst for creative destruction,
    208
identifying and capitalizing on, 7
micro-level impacts of, 198–199
1960s approach to, 9–10
profitability of, 55–56
traditional ways of practicing, 90
for value creation, 13–18
Capital intensity, 84–90
Capitalism, 63, 64, 199, 205
Carouselling, 154–155, 181–184
Cash flow deltas:
and capex budgets, 3–9
determining value from, 14–17
flawed thinking about, 18–21
to identify underperforming
    assets, 26
IRR calculations based on, 54
positive, 27
Cash flow(s):
accumulated discounted, 102–113
analysis using actual, 8
capex as percentage of EBITDA
    and, 86–87
capex projects and company, 3–9,
    89–90
company's ability to generate,
    83–84
maintaining or improving
    liquidity for, 24
negative net, 25, 26
operational, 80, 82–83
projected, 107–108, 145–151
from A sites, 38–39
valuation aspect of, 22–24
variable, 142–143
Cash flows for base alternative, 115,
    141–151
in base year, 143–145
and FTEs, 143

Cash flows for base alternative (*continued*)
and maintenance costs, 143
and overhead costs, 143
projected, 145–151
and SG&A costs, 143
variability in, 142–143
Categorization of production sites, 26–27, 42–43
CEOs:
as barriers to creative destruction, 205–206
in capex strategy teams, 95
China, free market forces in, 203–204
Clark, N., 183–184
Clearwater Paper, 181
Closing sites, 44, 158, 202
Closures, capacity, 162
Closure strategic building blocks, 160
Commodity industries, 77–78
Communication:
about ability to manage capital allocation decisions, 48
about value, 192
open, 95–96
Company governance, to execute RfA, 189–194
Company limits, 182–184
Company performance, 80–83
Company shares, buying back, 76
Competitive advantage, 76–77
Competitiveness:
from ability to invest in all sites, 60
industry, 34, 36, 73
measuring, 52
using BA to increase, 125
Computing power, 10–13
Concise recommendations for actions, 185–186
Consolidation, 60–64, 174–175, 201

Consumer companies, 77
Control, managerial, 100–102
Controllers to gather EBITDA split data, 141
Conviction, 11
Cost(s):
of capex projects, 155–158
of capital, 178
energy, 178
environmental cleanup, 202
fixed, 72, 141
labor, 61, 126, 178
of land, 61, 126
of M&As, 172–175
opportunity, 70, 74, 81
overhead, 141, 143
replacement, 133–136
SG&A, 141, 143
variable, 141, 142
COVID-19 pandemic, approaches to, 29–30
Creative destruction:
capex as catalyst for, 208
cultural barriers to, 204–205
declining markets and, 201
EBITDA margins and, 125
growth ambitions and, 200–201
institutional barriers to, 206–208
personal barriers to, 205–206
political barriers to, 201–204
Creative destruction funnel, 61–67
Cross-functional teams, holistic approach for, 8, 95
C sites:
categorization of, 26–27
investing in, 37, 38*t*, 65
management attention for, 39–40, 40*t*
Cultural factors:
in creative destruction, 204–205
in site closures, 158
Currency fluctuations, 179

Data collection:
  for capex strategy model, 98
  grassroots style of, 11
  shortcuts for, 134
Data quality, 16
Debate, allowing, 95–96
Debt, from previous capex projects,
  23
Decisions based on "gut feelings,"
  26
Delta cash flow curves, 109–113
Demand, market, 178
Deming, W. Edwards, 13, 128–129,
  197–198, 203
Depreciation, 52–53, 76, 88–89,
  174
Discounted paybacks, 5, 6, 109
Dividends, 76
Divisions, interdependent, 101
Domtar Corporation, 172
"Do Not Do!" slide, 187
Downstream operations, 77–78,
  87–88
Dynamic pricing, 162
Dynamics, of capex strategy model,
  121

Earnings before interest, taxes,
    depreciation, and amortization
    (EBITDA):
  calculating, 54
  capex as percentage of cash flow
    and, 86–87
  and capex needs, 172–173
  for capital-intensive companies,
    85
  controllers' data collection for, 141
  greenfield capex calculation to
    estimate, 18
  in less capital-intensive industries,
    85–86
  predicting future capex needs
    with, 174
  viewing, in isolation, 27

Earnings before interest and taxes
    (EBIT), 53
EBITDA cash flows, 143–145
EBITDA margin:
  assumptions about, 120, 125–128
  and base alternatives, 125–128
  to measure profitability, 52
Economic policy, creative
    destruction and, 203
Economic recovery, of Japan, 197–
    198, 204–205
Economics, 69, 73–74
Economic value, 71
Economy, capital allocation's impact
    on, 199
Efficiency paradox, 30–33
Energy costs, as systemic sensitivity,
    178
Engineering resources, project
    teams and, 132
Enterprise resource management
    software, 70–71
Enterprisewide analyses, 180–181
Environmental cleanup costs, 202
Environmental impact, of creative
    destruction, 199
Environmental regulations, BA and,
    125
Environmental sustainability, as
    systemic sensitivity, 179
European Union, green credits
    from, 202
Executive leadership, 95, 98
Expansion:
  creative destruction for, 198
  in declining markets, 201
  and growth in manufacturing,
    79–80
  organic, 76–77
  (See also Growth)

Financial crisis (2008), 178
Finished goods, 126
Fixed costs, 72, 141

Ford, Henry, 172
Free markets, 59–61, 126, 205
Free trade, 203
Full-time equivalent employees
    (FTEs), 141, 143

GM (General Motors), 30–31
Going concern principle, 57–67, 117
  and creative destruction funnel,
      61–67
  and macro-level economic
      forecasts, 59–61
  at SCA, 57–59
Google, 145
Gothenburg School of Economics, 58
Governance, company, 189–194
Green credits, 201–202
Greenfield capex calculation, 18
Growth:
  from consolidation, 64
  and creative destruction, 198,
      200–201
  in manufacturing, 79–81
  (See also Expansion)
"Gut feelings," decisions based on, 26

Harvard Business Review, 31
"Higher added value," 77
Holistic approach:
  to cross-functional teams, 8, 95
  to production, 7–9, 27
Homogeneous treatment, of
    production sites, 123
Howe, Art, 33
Human element, in strategic
    building blocks, 158–161
Hurdle rates, 74

Industry(-ies):
  consolidation, 60–61
  danger of seeing only your, 146
  individual performance vs.,
      average, 33–35
  (See also specific industries)

Inflation, 126–127
Infrastructure capex, 136–137
Innovation, as driver of creative
    destruction, 206
Inputs, variable costs of, 142
Institutional barriers, to creative
    destruction, 206–208
Insurance valuations, 136
Intermediary goods, 126
Internal pricing, 128–129
Internal rate of return (IRR):
  to measure value of capex projects,
      13–14, 57–58, 103
  in profitability measures, 46,
      53–55
Investments:
  planning for long term, 43–44
  profitability measures for, 55–56
  strategic, 153–154
IRR (see Internal rate of return)
Isolation, treating capex requests in,
    23, 27

Japan, economic recovery in, 197–
    198, 204–205

Labor costs, 61, 126, 178
Land, cost of, 61, 126
Landler, M., 183–184
Lawton, Toby, 43, 168
Leadership, 7, 97, 98
Ledgers, strategic asset, 137, 139
Legislation, BA and, 125
Lewis, Michael, 10–11
Limitations, 115, 182–184
Lindén, Daniel, 89, 203
Liquidity, 24
Local teams, in capex strategy
    teams, 97
Long-term capex plans, 8, 122,
    137

Machinery, maintaining, 85
Macro-level decisions, 32–35

Macro-level economic forecasts, 59–61

Maintenance, 85, 143

Management:
attention of, to categorized sites, 38–41
conflicts from control of, 100–102

Manufactured goods, price of, 61–62

Manufacturing, growth in, 79–81

Market-based internal pricing, 128–129

Market price, 120, 128–129

Market(s):
creative destruction and, 201
free, 126
interdependencies between, 101–102
serving existing, 124
systemic sensitivity and demand in, 178

Market shares, 79

Meadows, Donella, 131

Medium-term capex processes, 189–190

Mergers, cost of, 172–175

Micro-level decisions, 33

Microsoft Excel, 54

Miller, Christopher, 154

Mindset perspective for creative destruction, 206–208

Misallocated resources, 35–45
and Warren Buffet's investment, 42–43
and companies going bad, 43–45

Miscategorizing production sites, 42–43

*Moneyball* (Lewis), 10–11

National policies, 203

NBC, 42

Needs-driven capital budgeting process, 75

Negative net cash flow, 25, 26

Net present value (NPV):
capex and changes in, 20
and capital investments, 4
expansion to deliver positive, 79–80
as metric for capex analysis, 13–14, 103

Network of production sites, 93

*The New Economics for Industry, Government, Education* (Deming), 203

*New York Times,* 184

Nonproduction issues, capex strategy model and, 181–184

Nonrenewable outputs, 126–127

NPV (*see* Net present value)

Obsolescence, of sites, 60, 66

Ogilvy, David, 134

Open communication, 95–96

Operational age of assets, 132–133

Operational cash flows, 80, 82–83

Operations, downstream, 77–78, 87–88

Opportunity costs, 70, 74, 81

Opportunity-driven capital budgeting process, 75

"Optimizing Each Part of a Firm Doesn't Optimize the Whole Firm" (Satell), 31

Organic expansion, 76–77

Organizational perspective on creative destruction, 207

Ottoson, Erik, 58, 89

Outputs, of strategic asset mapping, 137–138

Overhead costs, 141, 143

Past performance, capital allocation decisions based on, 45–46

Payback:
discounted, 5, 6, 109
as a misleading term, 24–25

Payback period, 14, 66, 193

Performance:
of capex projects, 3–9, 82–83
industry average *vs.* individual
integrated systems, 33–35
maximizing company, 80–83
measuring, 52
Personal barriers to creative
destruction, 205–206
P&L (profit & loss) balance sheet-
based profitability measures,
46–53
Political barriers to creative
destruction, 201–204
Positive net present value, 79
Practicality, of capex strategic
model, 121
Predictive ability, of capex strategy
model, 121–122
Presentations, about RfA, 185–194
Price changes, as systemic
sensitivity, 178
Prices and pricing:
dynamic, 162
market-based internal, 128–129
of production, 141
Proactive approach to capex needs, 8
Production, as a holistic system,
7–9, 27
Production assets:
determining value of, 165
interdependencies between,
101–102
Production sites, *e.g.:* A sites), (See
also *specific categories*
categorization of, 26–27, 42–43
closing, 158, 162
equal treatment of, 120, 123–124
individualized slides for each,
187–189
networks of, 93
obsolete, 60, 66
reinvesting in, 51
specific cash flow models for each,
143

Production volume:
pricing, variable costs, and, 141
at A sites, 38
Product mix, assumptions about,
120, 124–125
Profitability index, 55–56
Profitability measures, 45–56
for capital investments, 47, 55–56
EBITDA margin to determine, 52
IRR, 53–55
P&L and balance sheet-based,
47–53
Profit and loss (P&L) based
profitability measures, 46, 47–53
Progress, capital allocation and, 208
Projected cash flows, 107–108,
145–151
Project team (PT), 99–100, 132

Quality, product, 125
Quality control, 71
Quality of life, 197

Raw material costs, 126, 178
Rebuilt assets, 133
Recommendations for action (RfA):
in capex strategy model, 115,
185–194
example of, 185–189
and governance, 189–194
presenting, 185–194
timeline for presenting, 100
Regulatory requirements, as
systemic sensitivity, 178
Reinvesting in sites, 51
Replacement cost, 133–136
Resource allocation, 35–45, 69–70,
83
Return on capital employed
(ROCE):
calculating, 49, 54
capex projects with high, 66
categorizing production sites
based on, 43

and EBITDA, 51
estimating past capex
performance with, 57–58
measuring profitability with, 47
RfA (*see* Recommendations for
Action)

SA (*see* Strategic alternatives)
Sabermetrics, 11, 12
Safety standards, BA and, 125
Samuelson, Paul, 69
Satell, G., 31
Sawmills, Swedish, 60, 62–64
SBBs (*see* Strategic building blocks)
SCA (forestry company), 43, 57–58,
83, 89, 146
Scenario analysis, 179–181
Schumpeter, Joseph, 63, 199
Scope, of capex projects, 100–102,
129
Selling, general, and administrative
(SG&A) costs, 141, 143
Sensitivity tests, 177–182
with capex-specific sensitivities,
177–178
and consistency of assumptions,
181–182
with systemic sensitivities,
178–179
and "What if?" scenario analysis,
179–181
SG&A (selling, general, and
administrative) costs, 141, 143
Share buy backs, 76
Shareholder value:
capex decisions and, 25
capital allocation and, 81–83
from capital allocation
opportunities, 87–88
market share *vs.*, 79
in markets with higher added
value products, 77–78
trust and ability to generate,
193

Short-term capex processes,
189–190
Site managers:
in capex strategy teams, 96–97
goal of capex projects for, 32
micro-level decision-making by,
33
Six Sigma, 13
Small-scale capex, 138–139
Smith, Adam, 126
Soviet Union. free market forces in,
203
Special treatment, of production
sites, 120, 123–124
Steinbrück, Peer, 184
Stora Enso, 75, 158, 192
Straight-line depreciation, 53
Strategic alternatives (SA), 115,
163–175
base alternatives for, 117
comparing, 108, 165–172
and cost of mergers and
acquisitions, 172–175
and timelines for capex strategies,
99, 100
Strategic asset ledgers, 137, 139
Strategic asset mapping for base
alternative, 131–139
and operational age, 132–133
outputs of, 137–138
and replacement cost, 133–135
and small-scale capex, 138–139
for structure and infrastructure
capex, 136–137
and useful life, 135–136
Strategic building blocks (SBBs),
115, 153–162
base alternative for, 117
and cost of capex projects,
155–158
human element in, 158–161
sensitivity tests for, 177
in timelines for capex strategies,
99

Strategic goals, of production
    systems, 59
Strategic intent, assumption of, 120,
    123
Strategic investments, 153–154
Streiff, Christian, 181–184
Structure capex, 136–137
Sustainable destruction, 197–208
    barriers to, 200–208
    benefits of, 198–200
    capex as catalyst for, 208
    cultural barriers to, 204–205
    growth and, 200–201
    institutional barriers to, 206–208
    market-based barriers to, 201
    personal barriers to, 205–206
    political barriers to, 201–204
System effectiveness, 32
Systems thinking, 29–56, 93–94
    about misallocated resources,
        35–45
    asset mapping with, 131
    for capex budgets, 9–13
    in COVID-19 pandemic, 29–30
    and efficiency paradox, 30–33
    and individual performance *vs.*
        industry average, 33–35
    new opportunities from, 90
    and profitability measures, 45–56

Tactical decisions, for production
    systems, 59
Tariffs, 203
Teamwork, 94–97
Technological advances, keeping up
    with, 34, 125
Terland, Ole, 146
*Thinking in Systems* (Meadows), 131
Three Levels of Contributors model,
    97
Time horizon, capex strategy, 117

Timelines:
    for creating and implementing a
        capex strategy, 98–100
    for restructuring capex strategies,
        109
Toeldte, Alexander, 181
Total shareholder return (TSR),
    3–5
Turnkey cost of project, 155–158

Underinvesting, 174
Underperforming assets, cash flow
    deltas and, 25
Universality, of capex strategy, 124
Upstream companies, 77–78

Value:
    destruction of, 69–70
    rescued, 22
    shareholder (*see* Shareholder value)
Value creation:
    acquisition of companies for, 165
    capex for, 13–18
    capital allocation for, 69–75
    and cash flows, 105–106
    creative destruction for, 199–200
    delta NPVs on capex and, 20
    metrics to determine, 13–18
Valukas, Anton, 31
Variable cash flows, 142–143
Variable costs of assets, 142
Vertical integration, 77

Waumbec Textile, 42–43
Weighted average cost of capital
    (WACC), 70, 74
Weissenrieder, Fredrik, 58–59, 89
Weissenrieder & Co., 98
"What if" scenario analysis,
    179–181
Williams, John, 172, 208

# ABOUT THE AUTHORS

When he was a graduate student at the University of Gothenburg's School of Economics and Law in Sweden, Fredrik Weissenrieder challenged his professors' assumption that the various metrics used to calculate capex analyses and measure profitability were somehow all related. He tried to write his master's thesis on the subject, but his professor wouldn't allow it: "There's nothing in the literature about this topic, Fredrik."

He finally found someone who would listen to his ideas instead of dismissing them out of hand: Erik Ottosson, the controller at the company that had inspired Fredrik's thesis. Together, they invented a completely new approach to corporate financial cash flow and created their own consultancy. While working with various companies, Fredrik was also invited to teach a class on the subject at the University of Gothenburg, which he did for three years. He also guest lectured in other classes. There, he met graduate student Daniel Lindén, who was studying industrial and financial economics. Thus their collaborative partnership began.

Realizing his passion focused solely on one aspect of their work, in 2004 Fredrik founded Weissenrieder & Co. together with Martin Wengblad, strictly dedicated to capex strategy consulting. In 2007, Daniel joined as COO and co-owner. After working with companies' capex teams for the better part of two decades and together having developed the capex strategy process to near perfection, Fredrik and Daniel saw that the software programs then available simply weren't up to the task. In 2015, they began developing a dedicated SaaS solution expressly for capital budgeting, capex management, and capex strategy—Weissr®, the wiser way to allocate capital.

Today, Fredrik continues in his role as CEO and chief spokesperson; Daniel serves in the dual roles of chairman of the board and COO, coordinating the firm's capex consultant teams as well as the tech teams developing the company's proprietary software solution. Both have consulted on capex strategy for some of the largest companies in their respective industries around the world.

Fredrik and Daniel are passionate about capex strategy because they recognize its potential to create a better world. They've witnessed firsthand the effects of creating more sustainable companies, both financially and environmentally. The two know of no better way to substantially move the needle on the world's challenges than becoming ever more effective at resource allocation.